Y0-CXG-397

DREADFUL CALIFORNIA

"Woman has come here not only to pander to man's vitiated appetites but also to create and foster in him unholier desires."

DREADFUL
CALIFORNIA

Being a true and scandalous account of the barbarous
civilization, licentious morals, crude manners and
depravities, inclement climate and niggling
resources, together with various other
offensive and calamitous details
of life in the Golden State

by

HINTON HELPER

edited by **LUCIUS BEEBE**
and **CHARLES M. CLEGG**

illustrated by **JAMES ALEXANDER**

THE BOBBS-MERRILL COMPANY
INDIANAPOLIS   *Publishers*   NEW YORK

CONTENTS

LIST OF ILLUSTRATIONS

DREADFUL CALIFORNIA

INTRODUCTION

Now and then in the course of recorded history there occurs or is perpetrated a hoax of such magnitude or such imaginative contriving that it achieves the status of legend. Some of these hoaxes familiar to students of the American saga have been devised in innocence of heart with no more sinister objective than the making of fools and gulls of a portion of the populace and for the laughter implicit in their success. More often they are invested with a fiduciary slant and are designed not only to make gulls of their victims but to do so to the considerable profit and enlargement of their authors. Neither of these two classifications of hoax is noted for the agreeable nature of its consequences. The practical humor type is apt to infuriate large numbers of persons and incite them to commit mischiefs of various proportions upon the originators. The fiduciary hoax usually even more infuriates its victims and incites them to greater and more resounding mischiefs upon the originators.

In the first of these categories there will be remembered the moment of whimsy which inspired the staff of James Gordon Bennett's *New York Herald* one

Sunday morning back in the seventies to startle the populace with the intelligence that the animals in the Central Park Zoo had escaped and were breakfasting in a highly informal manner off Sabbath strollers through the town's most celebrated plaisance. The burghers were urged to gather at the Fifty-ninth Street entrance armed with whatever weapons of approximate precision might be handy, and a notable concourse of deacons and other responsible burgesses appeared with an assortment of pikes, espontons and mangonels to excite the envy and interest of Francis Bannerman, the outfitter of South American rebellions. It was with difficulty that the mob was restrained from using this collection of antiquities upon the editors of the *Herald* when the lions were discovered safely in their cells at the zoo and all in good order with the tigers and panthers.

In a similar unfortunate vein was one of Mark Twain's more pointless and laborious inventions in the days when he was a member of the staff of Joe Goodman's *Territorial Enterprise* in Virginia City in the sixties. Thinking to make jape of the San Francisco papers for their lurid accounts of life in the Comstock, Mark Twain—in the pretentious and boozy manner which has somehow become confused in the general mind with a gift for inextinguishable humor—devised a horrid story of murder, madness and infanticide on the part of a Comstock citizen and it was run with full editorial substantiation in the *Enterprise*. In an age devoid either of laws of libel or even sense of propriety, he used the names of real people. The result of this tasteless satire was that it was universally reprinted as straight news. The characters listed in it as being either butchers or butchered were extremely cross, and it wasn't long thereafter that Clemens was being urged to leave Virginia City, preferably after dark and in a hack with drawn shutters.

In the category of financial hoaxes, probably the most famous in the American West was the matter of the great Nevada diamond mines of the seventies. In this almost stupefyingly childish swindle, a pair of bogus prospectors persuaded William Ralston, worldly and sophisticated president of the mighty Bank of California, that they had come upon a bonanza of diamonds, rubies, sapphires and emeralds of fantastic proportions in the Nevada desert, and produced a poke filled with rough gem stones to prove it. In no time flat the persons and organizations clamoring to be let in on the proposition included Shreve and Company, the conservative San Francisco diamond merchants, Tiffany and Company of New York, the Rothschilds of London, Horace Greeley, General George B. McClellan, John Hays Hammond, the foremost consulting engineer of his day, David Colton of the Southern Pacific Railroad and New York's super-conservative Samuel L. Barlow.

When the diamond fields were examined and found indeed to be rich in precious stones, some of them even going nature one better by being already cut and showing evidences of the lapidary art, Ralston restored nearly three million dollars in capital funds out of his own pocket to stockholders. The perpetrators of the hoax made off with a cool $660,000. The diamond mines of Nevada have been conversationally avoided in San Francisco's Montgomery Street ever since.

Celebrated, too, in the legend of sagebrush journalism in the Old West was that most scurrilous of all newspapers, the *Wabuska Mangler*. The *Mangler* was for many years a favorite source of editorial quotations in the exchange columns of the *Carson Appeal*, the *Territorial Enterprise* and other journals of wide repute and undoubted establishment. To be sure, nobody but other newspaper editors had ever seen a copy and no traveler—and they were infrequent—to Wabuska recalled having encountered it in circulation, but its editorials were widely quoted as examples of the fearful provocativeness of frontier editors. Nobody was safe from abuse and castigation in the *Mangler* and for years it enjoyed the reputation of being the man-eating tiger of Nevada journalism.

A particular Virginia City character of celebrated gun-fighting prowess was so outraged by references to himself attributed to the *Mangler* that he began preparing a one-man invasion of Wabuska with the purpose of assassinating the staff in its entirety. It was necessary for the *Enterprise* to chronicle that the proprietor of the *Mangler*, in terror of his life, had shut up shop and left for parts unknown. It was many years before it was generally known that there had never been a paper of any sort in Wabuska, let alone one of such famed ferocity as the *Mangler*.

With hoaxes of this magnitude for guidance and to serve as paradigms, does it seem remarkable that the people of America, and indeed of the entire world, should be made the object of a hoax whose almost cosmic proportions relegate the great diamond swindle to the category of the merest junior-high charade?

The hoax to which we refer and to the exposure and unmasking of which the author of this book dedicated himself is on such a gigantic scale that, at its merest contemplation, reason may well totter upon its throne. Its compass embraces a structure of purest fakement and chicane and to an incalculable multitude of unsuspecting believers it has been fobbed off as the very essence of verity itself. The innocent victims of its wanton falsification, fostered by indirection and direction too, must be beyond count or comprehension.

The hoax itself, staggering the human imagination with the dimensions of its scope and depravity, is, of course, the most monstrous and mischievous deception of the ages—the myth of California!

The origins of the great California imposture probably had their inception and sources in the fifties or sixties of the nineteenth century, although the person who fabricated their first and—as we now know through the agency of this volume—spurious accounts of its wealth, resources and potentialities remains shrouded in the mists of antiquity. Well may oblivion enfold his person! Suffice it to say that, perhaps in a spirit of innocent merriment, perhaps with the intention grossly to abuse the universal intelligence, the first California myth was born. Perhaps it concerned itself with that chimerical element, the so-called California climate. Perhaps its origin was the truly laughable beliefs in the fertility of the California soil, a fantasy which has persisted over the years despite the reports of recognized authorities from Texas and Florida to the effect that scarcely a square rod of its soil is indeed arable. Perhaps it contributed to the humorous delusion that in California it would one day be possible to wrest a living from its arts or manufactures, as though in this lonely and unproductive realm of desolation any of the fruits of communal industry could ever come to flower.

No matter; the idle fabrication, uttered for jape or malice, left its ever-crescent impress upon the gullible public consciousness until the myth of California had spread to the world's farthest reaches, transcending in its empty proportions all other delusions of modern times or even antiquity itself. So great is the human capacity for folly that it has been impossible to stay its progress or even to diminish the audacity of its pretensions.

In the course of ten decades only one single voice, literally crying in the wilderness, has been raised against this monstrous fabrication. Alone among the multitude, Hinton Helper has denounced the siren voices of chambers of commerce, has exposed their falsifications, has disproved their impossible statistics, perhaps the more effectively since he never encountered them. It has remained for Helper to rend the veil of hypocrisy from travel agencies and advertising campaigns, authors of guide and travel books and all the hucksters who traffic in nonexistent advantages, in wonderments of nature and civilization which, as this book so convincingly demonstrates, are not there!

It is indeed a fortunate circumstance that, although there have been other writers very numerous indeed who have, either for material reasons or from even more devious motives, been willing to contribute their share to the great myth of California, the resolution and discernment of Helper have prevented this monstrous legend from assuming even more lamentable proportions. Clearly he disabuses the minds of his readers of many of the superlatives which have been evolved in an attempt to persuade them to leave their established homes and substantial businesses elsewhere in the land and follow the will-o-the-wisp of fortune to the Pacific.

It may be noted for the record that, in one field alone, Helper is not unique in his sensations of outrage, and that is in his estimate of the depravity of civic character of San Francisco and the almost universal dementia of its inhabitants.

As distinguished an authority as Frederick Frohm, for a considerable period familiar to the San Francisco scene as "The Great Unknown," whose habit of wearing his hair down to his waistline earned him among the ignorant and unthinking the reputation of being an eccentric, supports Helper's estimate of the town's populace. "I have seen many cutthroats, horse stealers, gamblers and idlers and such like, but I never saw so many as I have met with here, and whisky shops at every corner."

Thirty years later, when San Francisco was a country town of almost georgic serenity compared with the sixties, Rudyard Kipling remarked, "San Francisco is a mad city, inhabited for the most part by perfectly insane people." In 1860 the *Alta California* itself said editorially: "It is really surprising to notice the great number of insane people who have been found in this city and provided for by the authorities. Hardly a day passes but the police are forced to take charge of some unfortunate persons laboring under an aberration of mind."

Allen Stanley Lane in his scholarly monograph on the Emperor Norton attributes San Francisco's high index of dementia to the lives led by pioneer gold seekers: "A life of hard work and no healthful social relaxation, of deprivation, restricted diet, lack of comfort, of lonely hours in tents or cabins far from home and family; of buoyant hopes shattered, more often than not, by cruel disappointment. To forget their troubles and drown their sorrows the miners often took to gambling and drinking. The result was frequently a demented mind."

All too clearly does Helper discern that even reason itself is not immune to the universal blight which he claims pervades every aspect of California's being!

Hinton Helper, no mere traveler and casual essayist, voyaged far and wrote unhesitatingly of vice and corruption wherever he encountered them, which appears to have been with gratifying frequency. *The Land of Gold*, which in the present edition is being published under the title of *Dreadful California*, was the first of a series of reports on his investigations into conditions which was to bring him fame of a sort. It was written when he was but twenty-five, but already it shows in emphatic detail not only his acute powers of observation but also his surprising command of language. If in

Dreadful California the author sounds old beyond his years, the reader will bear in mind that he has encountered, even if vicariously, many aspects of life popularly reputed to advance one's faculties more potently than the mere passage of time alone.

A native of North Carolina, Helper removed himself, as he chronicles so movingly, from his native clime in the first flush of youth. Later detractors have suggested that a shortage in his accounts of clerkship to a local merchant might have hastened his departure, but this may be discounted as the type of wanton defamation which must ever accompany success and fame of any sort in any age. That the suggestion of embezzlement or defalcation in his accounts was to crop up again in his later years but shows the lack of originality implicit in malice and the truth of the adage about giving a dog a bad name. In the latter case, when Helper was charged with a shortage in his accounts for the Federal government of a trifling six thousand dollars, it required no more than a change in the national administration and the election to the highest office of President U. S. Grant, a personal friend, to vindicate completely his good name and clear him of the absurd charges against his stewardship.

It can never be said of Hinton Helper that either personal inconvenience or the calumnies of detractors served to swerve his determination in the study of conditions and their exposure when it was merited. His report on conditions in the Deep South entitled simply *Impending Crisis in the South* appears to have been misunderstood so that after its publication it was inadvisable for him ever to return to his native North Carolina or the states of Lousiana, Mississippi, Alabama, Florida, Virginia, South Carolina, West Virginia, Georgia or parts of Arkansas, Texas and Missouri. The mere possession of this disputed tract once caused the hanging of three persons in Arkansas, this with due process of law.

It was at this period of Helper's career, when he was the subject of widespread editorial controversy and was even quoted in the halls of Congress, that the revival of the old charge of embezzlement from his former employer caused him to engage in a spirited fist fight with Congressman Burton Craige of North Carolina in a corridor of the House Office Building in Washington. When apprehended by the police Helper was found to be in possession of a Colt Navy revolver and a bowie knife of uncommon proportions and was remanded to the gow, although partisans pointed out that these items were as much a part of a gentleman's walking attire as his stick and gloves.

Later, after he had been released from the gow, he had an opportunity to study conditions among our Latin neighbors and the result was a book briefly entitled *Bolivia, as the Insidious Author and Perpetrator of a New International Crime*. This effectively eliminated portions of South America from any potential future itinerary.

It will be apparent to readers of his report on conditions in California as represented by the volume in hand, that it would be injudicious, subsequent to its publication, to reappear on the far side of the Sierras.

Every time he put pen to paper Helper cut down his future travel expenses.

It will be apparent from this brief chronicle of his encounters both of a personal and journalistic nature, that in Hinton Helper we find a social conscience which was afraid of nothing. His determination to study conditions brought him into conflict with public opinion throughout the Western Hemisphere, but the circumstance found him undaunted. Of physical opposition, whether it be in the form of congressmen, as noted above, or with four legged donkeys as will be discovered in his California adventures, he was also contemptuous.

In presenting this new edition of Helper's warning against the life of riot, license and peril which awaits those who venture to the furthest boundaries of our Western territories, the editors are constrained to point out that, for what seems to them sufficient reason, the original account of his expedition to California has been somewhat diminished in its volume and extent. Helper's complete account included considerable material descriptive of the westward passage as achieved by way of the Isthmus of Panama, but in view of the completion of the Pacific Railroad and the fact that California may now be reached with comparative expedition, if not safety, from Chicago in less than eight days, it was felt that this portion of his narrative might profitably be omitted.

For similar editorial reasons there have been one or two rearrangements of chapters and their titles, but in no place have any liberties whatsoever been taken with the text itself or with the spirit and intent of the author.

Helper's exposure of the great California hoax is an established classic in its field. It seemed, however, to the editors of this redaction of *Dreadful California* that its republication at the moment was more than justified by the existence of current conditions which would have aroused the crusading instincts of Helper himself. During the anniversary years of its gold exploitations and excitements, California will be at extra pains and efforts to lure to its boundaries an ever-increasing number of tourists and adventurers. The details of the California myth will be broadcast with an insidious persuasiveness never before practiced or imagined. Inducements will be devised to exploit the same sensuous and abandoned allurements of depravity from which Helper recoiled and against which he has taken so determined a stand. The year 1949 will, unless steps are taken, prove a centenary of licentiousness and corruption even as they were encountered by Helper.

He encountered them in 1852 and it was three years later that this book first saw the light of day.

L. B.
C. M. C.

CHAPTER ONE

CALIFORNIA
UNVEILED

An intelligent curiosity will find the history of few countries more interesting than that of California—which has at length realized those dreams of El Dorado that beguiled so many an adventurer from the comforts and bliss of his fireside, to delude and destroy him.

To explain the causes of frequent disappointment, to determine the true value of California and its principal cities, particularly San Francisco, and thus to enable those who still encourage golden dreams to form a proper estimate of their chances of success without submitting to the painful teachings of experience—these have been the motives which have actuated the author of the present work.

This book has been broken up into chapters in which the author proposes to discourse familiarly upon what he has seen and felt. In pursuing this plan, it is his intention to confine himself exclusively to facts and to describe those facts as clearly as possible.

In California, where almost every event that occurs

is as momentous and unaccountable as the wonderful exploits of Aladdin's genii, to deal with any thing aside from actual matters of fact is as silly and profitless as whistling against the wind. Yet in nine-tenths of the descriptions of life and times in California, truth and facts have been set aside and the writers, instead of confining themselves to a faithful delineation of that which actually exists, have made astonishing and unwarranted drafts upon their imaginations. Instead of detailing facts they have written fictions. They have chronicled dreams instead of realities and have registered vagaries as actual events and undeniable certainties.

They have been duped in listening to the delusive whispers of mischievous sirens whose flattering suggestions and plausible stories have had such a magical influence upon their excited minds that they have been converted to the belief that whatever California ought to be for their own particular ends and interests, it really is.

But the day will come, and it is fast approaching, when the spell must be broken. The iron utensils, which have been transmuted into golden urns and palaces night after night, shall once and for ever resume their true quality at the approach of day. The spell-bound shall be freed! The reverie shall be dissipated, the false wealth analyzed, and resolved into its component parts.

When these things are done, California will be seen in its true light. Then the eyes of the people will be opened. The golden haze which has hung over this land of romantic hopes and deadly disappointments will then be rolled away and the clear, naked sunlight of Truth will shine upon this ugly cheat, revealing it in all its naked deformity to the eyes of the abused and misinformed public. Then, and not till then, will the full extent of popular delusion on this topic be known, and this mighty genie collapse into its original caldron.

The truth is, California has been much over-rated and much overdone. Her managers have been rash, prodigal and incompetent, and they have embarrassed her beyond hope of relief. It must be acknowledged that California's condition was never very hopeful. She has never paid for herself. An overwhelming public debt now rests upon her shoulders and she has nothing to show for it. She is bankrupt.* Her resources are being rapidly exhausted, and there is but lank promise in the future. Her spacious harbors are not the easiest nor safest of access in the world as I shall hereafter prove by statistics of vessels wrecked upon this coast within the last six years. And before

---

* This unequivocal statement will at once put a stop to such mischievous rumors as that circulated by the California State Chamber of Commerce to the effect that incomes of individuals in California are the second greatest of all the states and in a single year approach the total of fourteen billions of dollars.

[27]

I finish I shall offer other information of interest and importance relative to the state at large.

I may remark here that, my curiosity having led me to collect and prepare this information with no little care and attention, and at no trifling sacrifice of time and means, it may be relied upon as correct.

A residence of nearly three years, during which time I have traveled over a wide extent of those parts of the State which are most highly esteemed for agriculture and minerals, has enabled me to arrive at a pretty accurate estimate of her character and capacities. I have no hesitation in avowing it as my candid opinion (and I have not been a very inattentive observer) that, balancing resource against defect and comparing territory with territory, California is the poorest State in the Union. She has little to recommend her except her fascinating metal.

I know it has been published to the world that this country possesses extraordinary agricultural abilities. This is an assertion wholly gratuitous and not susceptible of demonstration. Some of her valleys are exceedingly fertile, but when we compare their superficies with the area of the State we find they are but as oases in a desert. I seriously believe that a fair and thorough trial will show that she has more than three times as much sterile land, in proportion to her territory, as any of her sister states. On an average, a square rood of

Carolina earth contains as much fertilizing nutriment as an acre of California soil.

No rain falls between the first of April and the middle of November and the earth becomes so dry and hard that nothing will grow. The small amount of grass, weeds, or other vegetation that may have shot up in the spring is parched by the scorching sun until it is rendered as easy of ignition as prepared fuel. The valleys above mentioned are the only spots exempt from this curse. On the other hand, from the first of December to the last of March it rains so copiously and incessantly that all out-door avocations must be suspended. As there is no mechanical or in-door labor either of use or profit to be performed, the people are subjected to the disagreeable and expensive task of idling away their time in hotels and restaurants at the rate of from two to three dollars per day for board alone.

As for the valleys we have spoken of, they will afford a sufficient supply of breadstuffs to support sparse settlements, but the average or general surface of the country is incapable of sustaining a dense population.*

---

* This unqualified statement by Helper will go far toward disabusing any naïve belief in the statistics of the California State Chamber of Commerce which claim for California the largest gross annual income from farm products of any state in the Union and which rank it the first state in growth of grapes, oranges, peaches, pears, figs, dates, lettuce, asparagus, tomatoes and lemons.

If we inquire after the manufacturing and mechanical resources of the State, we will find that she has none whatever. Nor can she establish, encourage or maintain these arts for the reason that she would be under the necessity of importing not only the machinery and raw materials but also the fuel. She could not, therefore, compete with neighboring States which have at least some of these indispensable requisites. Nor has she any advantages or facilities for either water or steam power. How, then, can she obtain a reputation for manufactures and mechanism, having neither the material to work, nor the force or means to work with? She has neither cotton nor flax, coal nor timber. She is rich in nothing and poor in everything. She has to import every thing she uses and has nothing to export except her gold, which instead of being a blessing to her is a curse. Even the ground she cultivates has to be inclosed with imported fencing wire, not having timber suitable for railing or paling purposes.

That which is esteemed her chief treasure, dependence and commodity, gold, seems to be the least subservient to her advancement and prosperity for she sends it all away and retains none for home use. Thus it is that she has been a benefit to others while she has blindly and foolishly impoverished herself. In this she has acted upon the principle of the cobbler whose shoes are ever tattered, and of the blacksmith whose horses always go unshod.

But this profuse exportation of gold is significant of another important fact. It shows conclusively that there is no inducement to invest capital permanently in this country, either in the prosecution of business or in the establishment of homes or residences. Immigrants find neither beauty nor gain to hold them here and I feel warranted in venturing the assertion that not more than ten per cent of the population are satisfied to remain. Of the other ninety per cent, the bodies only subsist here—their hearts abide in better climes. They are anxiously waiting and wishing for the time when they shall have an opportunity of releasing themselves from the golden fetters which detain them and escape from a country which, with all its wealth, is to them a dreary prison.* Only a small minority of the few who are lucky enough, by fair means or foul, to accumulate fortune or competence, are induced to identify their lives and interests with the country.

The women are almost unanimous in their determination not to make California any thing more than a temporary residence and they have good reasons for this resolution. Besides the social depravity to which I shall presently allude, and which is sufficient to shock the sensibilities of any *man* of ordinary morality, there are hosts of minor annoyances that inflict peculiar pain

---

* According to the current census this indicates that in excess of seven million persons reside in California's dreary prison against their better inclination.

"The women are almost unanimous in their determination not to make California any thing more than
a temporary residence."

upon female sensibilities. The mud, which is often knee-deep, keeps them imprisoned all winter. In summer the dust, as fine as flour and as abundant as earth itself, stifles the inhabitants, fills the houses and penetrates into every nook and corner. It finds its way even into the inner drawers and chests, soils the wardrobe, spoils the furniture, and sullies everything. Besides, California is especially infested with vermin. Fleas, ants, and all sorts of creeping things are as ubiquitous as those that tormented Pharaoh and his people, and quite as annoying. No house is free from them.

As the ladies are the special sufferers from these abominable little nuisances, their unanimous dislike of the country is not at all to be wondered at. I can only offer the fact that I have yet to meet with one who is willing to make it her permanent abode.*

We have alluded to the winds, because they really are a peculiar feature in the meteorology of this State. In the summer time they blow with peculiar violence and facilitate the spread of the great fires from which California has suffered so much.

---

* This is substantiated by the widely celebrated exodus of elderly Californians who spend their declining years in Iowa.

CHAPTER TWO

SOCIETY IN
CALIFORNIA

Let us now briefly consider the moral and religious state of society in California. We know that we are undertaking an ungrateful and painful task—that we shall awaken the animosity of those who have an interest in enticing settlers and that we shall provoke contradiction—but we beseech Heaven to pardon us for speaking the Truth, and challenge our antagonists to disprove our statements.

We cannot pretend to disclose all the terrible iniquity of that society in the compass of a single chapter—the theme is too extensive, the facts too revolting. It requires space to unfold the scroll which records such damning facts and time is needed for the mind to become sufficiently reconciled to the hideous details, to be able to listen to them without impatience or disgust. Suffice it to say that we know of no country in which there is so much corruption, villainy, outlawry, intemperance, licentiousness, and every variety of crime, folly and meanness.

How much of this is attributable to the metal which attracts the population, we leave others to determine. It is certain, however, that gold mining districts do not generally enjoy a very enviable reputation in any part of the world and that they attract the most unthrifty and dissolute men who could not be induced to work at any thing else. Hence, the immediate neighborhood of a gold-mine is liable to be a sink for all the idleness and depravity of the surrounding country.

In the Atlantic States gold mining is only a branch of industry, and not a very important one compared with the other pursuits of the population. In California it is the chief occupation of the inhabitants of the mining districts. While in the former place the general virtue of the people keeps in check the particular vices of the miner, in the latter the good intentions of the few are overruled and stifled by the many.

We must not, however, commit the mistake of supposing that all the depravity of California is attributable to the nature of its industrial pursuits. This is but one of the elements which assist in producing the deplorable state of affairs under consideration. There are others which spring from the character of the people and the circumstances which brought them together.

It must be borne in mind that all the adventurers to this country have come for the express purpose of making money, and a large majority of them are of a class who are rarely troubled by any qualms of conscience. Mammon is their god and they will worship him.

Another very important cause of this wild excitement, degeneracy, dissipation, and deplorable condition of affairs may be found in the disproportion of the sexes—in the scarcity of women. The women are persecuted by the insulting attentions of the men, and too often fall victims to the arts of their seducers. Nowhere is the sanctity of the domestic hearth so ruthlessly violated as in California. For proof of this we need look no further than the records of the courts of San Francisco. They show that in the course of a single week no less than ten divorces had been granted, while during the same time only two marriages had been solemnized!*

Not long since, an English gentleman came to me requesting me not to let his wife draw any money from his account inasmuch as she had left him the day before. After finishing his business instructions, he gave us the following history. Listen to it. Said he: "Four years ago, myself and wife and six other men with their wives came together in one vessel to this country. Soon family feuds and jealousies became rife in the domestic circle of one of the parties. The man and his wife separated. Then their example was followed by another couple, and another, and so on, until all the mar-

---

* It will be seen that, at this rate of divorce and marriage, there will soon be left no married people to obtain divorces, which would probably cause a lot of confusion.

riage ties of our company were broken except those that happily existed between myself and wife. Having been true to each other so long I cherished the hope that we might remain together and be true to the end. But my fond thoughts and anticipations have proved a sickly dream. My hopes have been blasted, my happiness wrecked, and my children disgraced and deserted. My wife, whom I loved and held dearer than all else on earth, has been basely seduced. The last link that bound the remnant of our seven families together has been severed and we are a disbanded and disreputable people. Cursed be the day that started me to this damnable country!" These were his own words, almost verbatim, and he uttered them as if partly speaking to himself and partly addressing me.

The total disregard of the marriage tie by the majority of the men of California puts the husband, who is foolish enough to take his wife with him to that country, in a painful and embarrassing position. Should the wife be pretty, she is more liable to the persecution of attentions which will shock her if she be virtuous, and flatter her into sin if she is not. She is surrounded by hosts of men who spare neither money, time, nor art to win her affections from her husband. What wonder if they often succeed?

Female virtue or chastity is known to every one to be a very complex idea. There are women who are chaste only for want of the opportunity to be otherwise. There are others who are kept chaste by the force of public opinion, the dread of exposure and fear of the consequences. A third class preserve their persons untainted by an innate purity of soul which shrinks instinctively from all indelicacy and feels contaminated by an unclean thought, degraded by a lustful look. It is not our business to inquire into the relative proportion of women embraced in these three classes. It is enough to know that they exist, to appreciate the effect which the society of California will exert upon them.

As for the first class, it is not necessary to speak of them. They fulfill their shameful destiny every where and California only ripens their depravity a little earlier. It is the second class who suffer chiefly from the peculiar moral atmosphere of the land of gold. In the Atlantic States, hedged in by healthy public opinion, guarded by jealous laws and flattered into chastity by the respectful attentions which virtue commands, they might retain to their dying day that physical purity which satisfies the great majority of husbands. In California, however, these restraints are all removed. Public opinion arrays itself on the side of vice. The laws are powerless to punish the sins of impurity and all the attentions the women receive are based on the hope of their ultimate fall. How are such women to resist? Cut loose at once from all those restraints which kept them in the right way, they dart off into the devious paths of error and of sin. It is impossible that it should be otherwise.

The man who would keep faithful to himself a wife of this type in California must have wealth enough to gratify her most extravagant whims, time to devote exclusively to watching her, eyes keener than those of Argus and cunning sharper than that of Vidocq.

The third class—of whom, I regret to say, I have met with but few in the Eureka State—have also peculiar trials to undergo. Society in that country is a reproduction, on a large scale, of the morals of the courts of Charles II of England and Louis XV of France. Vice only is esteemed and lauded. Virtue is treated as an insulting pretence of superiority or a stupid folly beneath the notice of men of sense. People do not believe in it—they scorn it, they insult it. They consider it a mere avaricious attempt to dispose of venal charms above their market value. So the chaste woman has not only to suffer the persecution of insulting proposals but the doubt of that virtue which repels her pursuers, and the sneers and scandal of a depraved and debased community.

Many women of conceded respectability in California seem to have come out there for the exclusive purpose of selling their charms to the highest bidder. Others, of more honest hearts, have fallen victims to the peculiar seductions of the place.

But I must be allowed to pay a tribute to the sex. They have undoubtedly banished much barbarism, softened many hard hearts, and given a gentleness to the men which they did not possess before.

[39]

CHAPTER THREE

SAN FRANCISCO

WE WILL now pay our respects to the occidental metropolis of the United States, sometimes honored with the title of the Queen City of the Pacific.

It has not been more truthfully remarked that Paris is France than that San Francisco is California. It is the fountain-head of all the tributaries of trade and traffic that flow through the State and is the supreme tribunal and regulator of affairs. Every important movement, whether of a public, private, political or commercial character, receives its impetus from this point.

Owing to its advantageous geographical position, and the facilities and accommodation offered for shipping, I think it may be safely said that San Francisco will be a great city, although California can never become a great State.

Let us, in order to furnish the reader with a more systematic idea of the city, imagine ourselves in a vessel approaching the coast of California through the Golden Gate, the entrance to the harbor. This entrance is a narrow outlet which can be so thoroughly fortified that no maritime expedition could ever force its way through it.

Passing through the Gate, we enter the bay and find it to be one of the largest and finest in the world, dotted with several small islands, and abounding in excellent fish of every variety. Soon we arrive at Long Wharf. The steamer is run alongside, and we are in the El Dorado of modern times. Around us we behold an innumerable crowd of eager lookers-on who have come down from the city to meet the ship. The crowd is probably one of the most motley and heterogeneous that ever occupied space. It is composed of specimens of humanity from almost every clime and nation upon the habitable globe. We see all grades and conditions, all ages and sexes, all colors and costumes, in short, a complete human menagerie.

By the sides of the wharves, and anchored in different parts of the commodious and noble bay, we see magnificent ships, barks and brigs from every nation of commercial note. But of all these majestic palaces of the deep, none are equal in beauty of design and finish, in grace, symmetry and elegance, or in excellence of quality, to our own American clippers.

Leaving the vicinity of the shipping, we wend our way towards the heart of the city. Degradation, profligacy and vice confront us at every step. Men are passing to and fro with haggard visages and heads declined, muttering to themselves and looking as hungry and ferocious as the prowling beasts of an Asiatic jungle. Before us on either side we see a group of boys clad in slouched hats, dirty shirts, ragged pants, and shabby shoes without socks, who have no regular business*

At this time several of them seem to have met by chance and they have stopped to discuss the times and the progress of events. If we were near enough we should probably hear the right hand party criticising Madame Anna Thillon's last performance of the opera of La Somnambula, or of the Daughter of the Regiment, and those on the left giving their opinions upon the merits of Madame Anna Bishop's last oratorio or ballad concert. After disposing of all the actors and actresses in music, opera, pantomime, tragedy and comedy, or after bragging of the successes of certain amours or other youthful depravities, they rally together, and entering the nearest groggery one calls for a brandy smash, another for a whiskey punch, a third for a gin cocktail, and so on until all are served. Then, bowing to each other they drink to the prosperity of Young America, and dashing their glasses upon the counter with as hideous and vociferous anathemas as ever passed the lips of an East India

---

* Should these be classified as the lineal antecedents of zoot suiters or are they more properly the forerunners of the bobby-soxers?

pirate, they separate, segar in mouth, and return to their respective avocations.

Not unfrequently these vicious youths repeat their potations so often that they become thoroughly inebriated and may be seen quarreling, fighting, and lying about the streets like hardened and inveterate topers.

The bales and stacks of hay and straw piled upon some of the wharves deserve a passing glance since they form the sleeping apartments of dozens of penniless vagabonds who are always wandering about the city in idleness and misery. They have no other place to rest, no bed except these out-door packages of provender into which they creep for shelter and slumber during the long hours of the night.

Continuing our perambulations in a westerly direction, we find ourselves at the foot of Commercial Street, which runs almost due east and west through the center of the city. Let us walk along this street. The houses are from one to two stories in height, and are built of red wood, a very light combustible kind of timber, imported from Oregon.

Higher up the street we come to a better class of buildings than the miserable little shops we have just left, and we get a fair view of the permanent and attractive architecture of San Francisco—the brick and stone structures. Many of these buildings are beautifully designed and symmetrically proportioned, and have fire-proof walls varying from sixteen to twenty-four inches in thickness. They are usually from two to four stories in height. One hotel is five stories high, being the tallest house in the State.*

Probably no city in this country can boast of buildings so substantial and thoroughly fireproof as those of San Francisco. Besides making the walls very thick, every care is taken to have the doors, window-shutters and roofs equally stout and incombustible. Nor is this precaution at all surprising when it is remembered that this city alone has lost more than twenty-five millions of dollars by fire.

Owing to the unusual dryness of the weather, the prevalence of winds in summer and the inadequate supply of water possessed by the city, all combustible matter is rendered so inflammable that it is quite impossible to keep it from burning after fire is once communicated; hence the necessity of using brick and stone instead of wood. The amount of money invested in this durable kind of improvement is something over thirteen and a half millions of dollars—the number of buildings being six hundred and thirty-eight.

It is a remarkable fact, however, that less than half of these improvements have been made with California gold. Ask the proprietors where they got the money which they have expended in the erection of

---

* Could this be a reference to the Mark Hopkins Hotel?

these buildings and they will tell you it came from the Atlantic States and from Europe. Those who occupy them, the merchants and business men from New York, London, Paris, and other places, will testify to this fact.

These buildings are erected upon the most eligible and convenient sites and form what is properly termed the business portion of the city—covering, probably, about one-sixth of its superficies. Almost all of the residences or private dwellings are built of wood, and are very frail and inelegant. It is the intention, however, of a large number of the citizens to take down the wood and substitute brick or stone as soon as they get able, if that is ever to be the case.

To acquaint ourselves with the character of the speculators and business men in San Francisco would be a curious and interesting task. They are certainly the shrewdest rascals in the world, and a straightforward, honest man, who acts upon principle and adheres to a legitimate system of dealing, can no more cope with them than he can fly. But notwithstanding their shrewdness, and I might say in some instances, their excellent business qualifications, they exhibit less method and system in their transactions than any class of traders I ever saw. Whatever they do is done in a helter-skelter, topsy-turvy sort of way, as if they had just fallen out of their element and were scrambling to get back again. They never take time to do a thing well but are always bustling about in such a manner that one would suppose they were making preparations for some calamitous emergency, rather than attending to the every day routine of an established occupation. This restless disposition is characteristic of the inhabitants of every part of the State.

It may be remarked that San Francisco is no longer dependent upon the State for her support. San Francisco can now claim to be as much the city of the world as of California. The commercial advantages she enjoys, her inviting harbor and central position, are far superior in importance to any benefit she is likely to receive from the interior. The profits she will gain from the whale-fishing fleet of the North Pacific, and from her trade with the islands of the South Pacific, with China, Oregon and Russia, will place her in a more prominent and enviable position than it is possible for the State ever to attain.

Returning to our subject, we find ourselves as far advanced on our way as Montgomery street. The course of this street lies north and south through the middle of the most beautiful and wealthy part of the city. It is, therefore, both the Broadway and the Wall street of San Francisco. Every phase and trait of life and character is cognizable here. The dramatist who would study human nature here would have an opportunity of striking out something new, instead of

"Lawyers have been compelled to fish around
the wharves for crabs."

repeating the old creations of his predecessors, for surely never was there so varied a page spread out before the eyes of man.

While in this vicinity we may observe men, who in the Atlantic States bore unblemished reputations for honor, sinking into the lowest depths of shame and degradation. Others, whose moral characters are unobjectionable, have been pecuniarily unfortunate and are driven to the necessity of engaging in the most menial and humiliating employments. Among the latter class I might mention lawyers, who to save themselves from the severe pangs of actual want, have been compelled to fish around the wharves for crabs and to enlist themselves in the petty traffic of shrimps and tomcods. Ministers and physicians fare no better. In a certain hotel in this city not long since, a lawyer was employed as a regular runner. In another, adjacent to it, a physician was engaged to pare potatoes and wash dishes. In a neighboring restaurant, a preacher was hired to wait on the customers and clean off the tables. Now every reasonable man knows that these professional men did not voluntarily follow these inferior pursuits. It was not a matter of choice with them. They couldn't help themselves. They were out of money, destitute of friends, and were compelled to take advantage of the first opportunity that offered.

New as the country is, the dandy, that exquisite flower of a finished civilization, is not unknown. He may be seen at any time sunning his external splendor on the side-walk and scorning his more useful contemporaries as loftily as though he were promenading Broadway or the Champs Elysées.

Together with bankers, stock-jobbers, and other moneyed men, we observe that the students or disciples of Blackstone, Coke and Story have selected this street for their offices. Considering the heterogeneous composition of society in this country, the loose and unsystematic transactions of every-day business, and the unsettled state of public affairs, it will be readily perceived that there is a great deal of strife and litigation. Disputes and difficulties relative to real property, and spurious or imaginary claims, keep the court dockets continually crowded.

Some of the lawyers have been more fortunate in accumulating wealth than any other class of men. Much of their business has been of such a nature that they could mould it almost exclusively to their own interest, and everybody knows it would be a very unlawful thing in a lawyer to neglect himself. They are the largest owners of real estate in the city and there is no species of property that yields so great a profit as this, if properly managed.

Land titles are now as much contested as they ever were, there being in some instances as many as half a dozen claimants to a single lot. If the law were sufficiently forcible—if there were any such thing in California as sovereign law, these intruders would be brought to justice. But as it is, no dependence can be placed upon the administration of justice and unless a man takes the law in his own hands, and defends his person and property *vi et armis*, he must tamely submit to whatever injury or indignity is offered him.

The grog-shops or tippling-houses constitute the last but not the least prominent feature of Montgomery street that we will notice at the present time. The devil has certainly met with more than usual success in establishing so many of these, his recruiting officers, in this region. We cannot visit any part of the state or city without finding them always at our elbow. San Francisco might allot one to every street corner in the city, or in other words, four to every intersection of the streets, and still her number would not be exhausted.* It is astonishing what an amount of time, labor and money is misspent in this nefarious traffic. Out of the two hundred and fifty thousand inhabitants in California, from twelve to fifteen thousand are exclusively engaged in this diabolical but lucrative business.

And what is worse, nearly one-fourth of the bars

---

* There is, of course, a well-established school of thought which holds that Dublin, Ireland, maintains more drinking resorts per capita of population than any city in the world. This heretic thesis has been indignantly denied by Angelo Rossi, a recent San Francisco mayor, within the hearing of the editors. "HELPER IS RIGHT!" asserted Mayor Rossi without hesitation. "SAN FRANCISCO HAS MORE SALOONS."

are attended by young females of the most dissolute and abandoned character, who use every device to entice and mislead the youthful and unsuspecting. Women being somewhat of a novelty here, their saloons are always thronged with customers, many being induced to patronize them merely for the sake of looking at them. What a base prostitution of their destiny and mission! Woman has come here not only to pander to man's vitiated appetites but also to create and foster in him unholier desires.

Lest we should fall in love with one of these sirens, we will not go near them, but will enter one of the saloons kept by one of our sex. Across the street is a large and fashionable one, called the Blue Wing,

"Where politicians most do congregate,
To let their tongues tang arguments of State."

Adding ourselves to the number of its inmates, we find the governor of the State seated by a table surrounded by judges of the supreme and superior courts, sipping sherry cobblers, smoking segars and reveling in all the delights of an anticipated debauch.* Another group occupies a second table in the back part of the room where they are playing cards and carousing over

---

* A close parallel to this unsavory circumstance may be found in the record of the days when the Senate of the State of Colorado foregathered for its official deliberations in the bar room of the Windsor Hotel in Larimer Street.

"We find the governor of the State seated by a table surrounded by judges of the supreme and superior courts."

a general assortment of distilled, fermented and malt liquors.

The proprietor himself is a red-nosed, jolly fellow of burgomaster proportions who treats his victim-patrons with the utmost courtesy and politeness. He is every man's man, and always has a smile and a smart saying prepared for the entertainment of the by-standers. His two clerks are equally urbane in their deportment and may be found at their posts from six o'clock in the morning ready to flavor and tincture mixed drinks, to prepare hot punches, and to deal out low anecdote to vulgar idlers. On the shelves and counters are dozens of labeled decanters and bottles filled with the choicest liquors and artificial beverages that the world produces. As minute survey of the bill of fare may be interesting, I herewith present it:—

BILL OF FARE OF A CALIFORNIA GROGGERY.
Bowie Knives and Pistols.

Scotch Ale,
English Porter,
American Brandy,
Irish Whiskey,
Holland Gin,
Jamaica Rum,
French Claret,
Spanish Sack,
German Hockamore,
Persian Sherbet,
Portuguese Port,
Brazilian Arrack,
Swiss Absynthe,
East India Acids,
Spirit Stews and Toddies,
Lager Beer,
New Cider,
Soda Waters,
Mineral Drinks,
Ginger Pop,
Usquebaugh,

Sangaree,
Perkin,
Mead,
Metheglin,
Eggnog,
Capilliare,
Kirschwasser,
Cognac,
Rhenish Wine,
Sauterne,
Malaga,
Muscatel,
Brandy Smashes,
Whiskey Punch,
Cherry Bounce,
Shamperone,
Drizzles,
Our Own,
Red Light,
Hairs,
Horns,

Whistler,
White Lion,
Settler,
Peach and Honey,
Whiskey Skin,
Old Sea Dog,
Peg and Whistle,
Eye Opener,
Apple Dam,
Burgundy,
Haut Bersae,
Champagne,
Maraschino,
Tafia,
Negus,
Tog,
Shambro,
Fisca,
Virginia,
Knickerbocker,
Snifter,
Exchange,
Poker,
Agent,
Floater,
I O U,
Smasher,
Curacoa,
Ratafia,
Tokay,
Calcavalla,
Alcohol,
Cordials,
Syrups,
Stingo,
Hot Grog,
Mint Juleps,
Gin Sling,
Brick Tops,
Sherry Cobblers,
Queen Charlottes,
Mountaineers,
Flip Flap,
One-eyed Joe,
Cooler,
Cocktails,
Tom and Jerry,
Moral Suasion,
Jewett's Fancy,
Ne Plus Ultra,
Citronella Jam,
Silver Spout,
Veto,
Deacon,
Ching Ching,
Sergeant,
Stone Wall,
Rooster Tail,
Vox Populi,
Tug and Try,
Segars and Tobacco.

The annual consumption of beer, wines and liquors in this State exceeds five millions of gallons, and it is retailed at extraordinarily remunerative rates. All of the first class establishments charge twenty-five cents for every delicious (?) draught they sell.

I may not be a competent judge, but this much I will say, that I have seen purer liquors, better segars, finer tobacco, truer guns and pistols, larger dirks and bowie knives, and prettier courtezans here, than in any other place I have ever visited; and it is my un-biased opinion that California can and does furnish the best bad things that are obtainable in America.

We will now look into Clay street, which intersects Montgomery. Next to Montgomery, this is the most fashionable street in the city, the large establishments where retailers deal in ladies' and gentlemen's dress goods being situated upon it. The side-walks are narrow and generally crowded to such an excess as to render it really difficult and tiresome to travel them. To the ladies, shopping on this street is especially annoying and tedious, for they are designedly balked or hindered in their course by a set of well-dressed vagabonds who promenade the *trestoir* from morning to night for the sole purpose of staring in their faces.

The gambling-houses cannot be overlooked in a true sketch of life in San Francisco. One of the largest and most frequented of these, called the Diana, stands a few doors above us. The building extends through the entire block from Clay to Commercial street and has a front proportionate to its depth. The doors which lead into it from either street are kept wide open from nine in the morning and the hall or saloon is generally filled to overflowing with lazy men of little principle, whose chief employment consists in devising some sinister plans of procuring a livelihood without work.

On one side is a bar attended by a *lady*, assisted by three young white men and two negroes. This is patronized by the occupants of the saloon—one-fifth of them drinking because they have been lucky and the other four-fifths drinking because they have been unlucky. Around the walls are suspended showy paintings and engravings, some of them the very size of life, representing nude women in every imaginable posture of obscenity and indecency.

The proprietor of the house rents his gambling-tables to professional gamblers at a stipulated sum per month with the condition that he is to receive a certain per centage on the net proceeds of their swindling operations. Usually two gamblers form a co-partnership, hire one table, and station themselves opposite each other so that each can understand every manoeuvre and secret sign of the other. When a good opportunity for cheating or defrauding presents itself to one of them, the other is always prepared to divert the attention of the victim from his partner's motions. Every possible variety of gaming that can be accomplished by cards and dice is practiced here and every false and dishonest trick is resorted to to fleece ignorant men of their money.

Lying on the top of each table is a pile of gold and silver coin called "the bank," the size and amount of which depend altogether upon the wealth of the proprietors. I have said "the bank" is composed of gold and silver coin. It must be one or the other, or both of these metals in some shape—whether in dust, ingots, bullion, or coin,* since there are no bank-notes or paper money in circulation.

At one of the tables we observe two proprietors. One of them is a lank, cadaverous fellow with a repulsive expression of low cunning, full of hypocrisy and deceit, taciturn in disposition, unengaging in manners, who was formerly a Baptist preacher in Connecticut.** The other has a fat and jolly coun-

---

* An inconvenient practice to which, when he was informed of it, an end was put by the late President Franklin D. Roosevelt.

** The number of clerics fallen from grace in the California scene is attested by numerous other trustworthy writers.

"In the Bella Union (a gambling parlor of universal note) might be seen a man about fifty years of age, rather above medium height with a refined, intellectual face, forehead, high broad and white; gray, neatly combed hair worn rather long; white cravat and black suit," wrote Barry and Patten in *Men and Memories of 1850*. "This individual presided with quiet and unruffled dignity at the very interesting but baffling enigma known as Faro—*genus felis tigris*. The courteous gravity with which he witnessed the fluctuations of the game and the undisturbed serenity of his benign features, through heavy

tenance, enjoys a joke and laughs at his partner for being so melancholy. He is affable and courteous to strangers, talks a great deal as might be expected since, before he came to California, he was considered one of the most promising young lawyers in Mississippi.

The proprietors of another table are two old gentlemen of "three score years and ten," whose white hairs and wrinkled brows would seem to belong to a more honorable station in life.

A third table is used by a couple of Spaniards whose scowling brows and treacherous eyes indicate that they are better qualified for the transaction of infamous and atrocious deeds than for fair dealing or magnanimous behaviour. A Jew and Jewess have

---

loss or high success, was always a study for the physiognomist and observer of human nature.

"One afternoon a grave looking man and clerical in appearance stopped in his stroll through the crowded saloon. . . . Happening to raise his eyes, he, the object of our study . . . looked upon the clerical looking man. A keen observer might have detected a slight start, a sudden but faint flush upon the face of the all-unconscious dealer, but it was scarcely discernible and the next moment the face was placid and self-possessed as usual. When the deal was finished, the dealer rang a bell . . . spoke quietly to the attendent servant who returned with an assistant, and the game proceeded as usual.

"Meanwhile he who had left the chair walked leisurely out of the room to the open plaza, first giving the clerical looking man an indication of the head toward the door. In a moment the two were in close and earnest conversation which lasted some time. The purport of that conference was never known; but many of the 'Sports' from Alabama and Mississippi surmised its nature, as they had known both gentlemen as eloquent preachers in the Methodist Church South."

command of the fourth table. The fifth is under the direction and management of a French *gentleman* and *lady*. A young American girl and her paramour have charge of the sixth, while the seventh, eighth, ninth, tenth, and so on, are presided over by sundry sorts of wicked spirits unworthy of being named.

Here, youthful and middle-aged men, women, boys and girls, white and black, brown and copper-colored all associate together and as might be expected, fight, maim, and kill each other with the same indifference with which people generally pursue their daily occupations.

There is generally erected a stage or platform upon which a company of musicians perform at intervals of a quarter of an hour. This they are employed to do for the purpose of enticing in unsuspecting strangers and passers-by.

Like those engaged in the liquor traffic, these gamblers are a public nuisance and yet the community grants them a license to abuse the public and to debase themselves.

Thousands of these swindlers live by their expertness in gambling and tricks of legerdemain. Dissipated, reckless, and restless, they rove from place to place rarely acquiring decent habits or becoming permanent citizens. They are, nevertheless, great lovers and admirers of women. Most of them make it a special branch of their business to cultivate a due share of female acquaintance. But we will now bid adieu to the blacklegs and return again to the street, merely stopping a minute or two as we pass out, to listen to the enchanting strains of "Katy Darling," or "Lilly Dale," played by the brass band in attendance.

The plaza, or park, which occupies one square between Washington, Clay, Kearney and Brenham streets now lies before us. As it is nothing more nor less than a cow-pen inclosed with unplaned plank, we will say but little about it. In the middle is planted a tall liberty-poll, near which is erected a rude rostrum for lynch-lawyers and noisy politicians. If there is a tree, or a bush, or a shrub, or a sprig of grass, or anything else in or about it that is green, or that bears the slightest similitude to vegetation, nobody has ever yet seen it. As a pleasure-ground, it is used only by the four-footed denizens of the city.

On the east side of this delectable public square is the California Exchange, before the steps of which are stationed from fifteen to twenty French peasants who pursue no business save that of blacking boots. Most of them have acquired or adopted this ornamental occupation since they left La Belle France.

A few doors above the Exchange stands the City Hall which was formerly the Jenny Lind Theatre—a very neat stone structure but wholly unsuited for the purpose to which it is now applied. The parties who built it for a theatre soon ascertained that it was a bad speculation, and became considerably involved in debt. To save themselves and make the best of a bad bargain, they bribed a majority of the aldermen to purchase it for a City Hall at thousands of dollars above the original cost. They consummated their corrupt bargain for the theatre, the properties were removed and after the expenditure of much time, labor, and money, in making alterations and additions, the building was converted into what now stands before us—the City Hall of San Francisco.

This is a fair sampe of the disposition that is made of the public funds throughout the State. Sheriffs, treasurers, and tax-collectors, in the majority of cases, are expected to decamp with all the money in their hands, or to embezzle part. It has passed into a proverb that no *honest* man can be elected to a city, county, or state office in California.

Were we to remain an hour or two in this vicinity, we should probably see a police officer rolling a lady in a wheelbarrow. Intoxication is quite common among the ladies of this particular section of San Francisco, and the wheelbarrow or some other vehicle must be employed to convey them to the station-house on account of the total failure of their natural organs of locomotion.

On the north side of the Plaza are some of the best French eating-houses in the State. One of them, the *Café du Commerce,* which translated means Commer-

"Intoxication is quite common among the ladies of this particular section of San Francisco."

cial Coffee-house, is quite famous for its choice gastronomy. A better dinner can be procured here than in an American house because the French are better cooks, cleaner, more polite and attentive to their guests and less accustomed to adulterating their provisions. Dinner, without wine, costs two dollars for each person, but with it, from three to five dollars according to quality and quantity consumed.

The stranger cannot promise himself any thing very sumptuous or delicious in the way of eatables in the first-class hotels. He can get good wines and liquors, prime segars and tobacco, and other accessory articles of superior quality, but the fare at best is very indifferent.*

All the more substantial articles of food, such as flour, meal, beef, pork, and butter, are imported from Europe or brought from the Atlantic States. As these provisions are sent around by Cape Horn, they must pass twice through the tropics before they arrive in San Francisco and consequently most of them become more or less sour, musty, or rancid. Old or fresh, sound or unsound, they must be sold, served up, cooked, eaten. They cannot be wasted or thrown away for that would be a losing business and people did not come to California to lose money, but to make

---

* This should put an end to the fanciful tales of returning voyagers concerning the Oysters Kirkpatrick and Roulade of Sand Dabs at the Palace Hotel.

it. Sour flour is sold at reduced prices to the bakers, who mix it with a larger quantity—say twice as much —of that which is sweet. Then it is manufactured into bread.

Within the last one or two years, considerable quantities of the cerealia have been cultivated in the low lands and valleys of this State, and a few flour mills have been erected which are now in operation. However, they mix their grists so much with rye and barley that the flour is less marketable than it would be if it was ground out of genuine wheat. To give character to their spurious compound they pack it in empty Gallego and Haxall barrels which are clandestinely purchased and kept in readiness for the purpose. Though the fraud is easily detected when the barrels are opened, there is no chance of obtaining redress because in California it costs more to adjust a wrong by law than it does to endure it.

This system of cheating and adulteration is carried out in all ramifications of business. If a man is not continually upon the alert he is sure to suffer the penalty, and that without redress.

To return from our digression. Although the French are somewhat more philosophic and scientific in their preparation of viands, we perceive no material difference between their mode of living and our own. They eat more slowly, are more graceful in their deportment at table, and seem to enjoy their meals as a feast rather than as a necessary repast.

Wine is their principal drink, morning, noon and night. Dinner to them without it, would be as insipid and unpalatable as breakfast to our American grandmothers without coffee. After the main part of the meal is finished it is customary with them to sip a small cup of strong coffee as a sort of accompaniment to their dessert. This, however, they do not flavor with cream, but use Cognac, burnt with sugar, instead. It is an unusual thing for them to drink water at any time except when mixed with wine. I have the pleasure of the acquaintance of a very worthy French gentleman who assured me that he had taken but one drink of crude water in four years, "and then," he added, "it make me sick."*

---

* This unfortunate contingency may be avoided by the practice of an uncle of one of the editors who followed a lifelong habit of brushing his teeth with a light Moselle, thus eliminating the possibility of swallowing even the smallest quantity of emetic substance.

CHAPTER FOUR

SAN FRANCISCO—
CONCLUDED

AFTER a night's lodging in one of the human-stables of San Francisco, called here for politeness' sake, hotels, we felt sufficiently refreshed to continue our reconnoissance of the city. It will probably be well for us to retrace our steps to the south side of the Plaza where we re-enter Clay street and ascend the long, high hill that forms the western boundary of the city.

Before proceeding far we come to a pistol gallery on the left, owned and conducted by one Dr. Natchez, a short, thick-set "son of thunder" who keeps on hand the best assortment of dueling apparatus that the world affords. The proprietor's real cognomen is Brown, but everybody calls him Natchez because he came from the town of that name in Mississippi. He knows all about guns, pistols, and ammunition. He's an excellent shot—can hit a man's eye every time he pulls a trigger, and never fails to vindicate his honor when it is assailed.

"There is no one so capable of giving suitable advice
or so well prepared to supply the necessary instru-
ments of polite slaughter."

There is no one so capable of giving suitable advice
or so well prepared to supply the necessary instru-
ments of polite slaughter as Dr. Natchez.

Among the fiery spirits of this Western Metropolis,
the slightest affront, even though it may be purely

[67]

accidental, is considered a wound to dignity curable only by an application of a Colt's revolver to the breast of the transgressor.

As Dr. Natchez enjoys the reputation of preparing the best remedies for wounded honor, all those afflicted with the disorder apply to him for relief. Laying before him their ailments and grievances, he will at once say "the cause must be removed" and the Doctor, with commendable impartiality, superintends the preparation of the weapons for both parties.

Passing on towards the summit of the hill before us, we soon arrive at an elevation from which we have a clear and uninterrupted view of the whole city, which contains about fifty thousand inhabitants. The original water-boundary of the city on the bay at the east was in the form of a crescent, but the bay being shallow in this particular part, its shape has been changed by filling it in with sand from the adjacent hills. The land thus made, to the wharves, is far more valuable than that of natural formation. At first, however, heavy losses were sustained in consequence of the insecure foundations of most of the buildings, some of which gave way entirely. Now, however, they understand it better and take special care to pile and plank the foundation thoroughly before the superstructure is erected.

The process of filling up these water-lots was very irregular and as the work advanced several ponds of water, which afterwards became stagnant, were cut off from the ocean. In other places the tide receded from the shallow parts of the bay and from the surface left bare, as well as from the ponds last mentioned, there arose large quantities of highly offensive and almost suffocating gas which obliterated all the painted signs in the immediate vicinity.

Viewing the city from our present elevated position, we look in vain for any verdure. Indeed, there is not a shade-tree in San Francisco. The earth all around us is as sterile and unproductive as a public highway. Here nature wears a repulsive and haggard expression. I entertain no doubt that a large, luxuriant elm would attract more attention in San Francisco than a menagerie or circus, and it is a wonder that some ingenious Yankee has not manufactured one out of soft pine and dyed muslin for public exhibition.

A distinguished gentleman with whom I recently had the honor to dine said to me (his wife at the time being in North Carolina), "I long for the society of trees almost as much as I do for that of my wife, and if she and a big oak could now be placed side by side within my reach, I scarcely know which of the two I should embrace first!"

CHAPTER FIVE

CALIFORNIA CELESTIALS

THE national habits and traits of Chinese character, to which they cling with uncompromising tenacity in this country, are strikingly distinct from those of all other nations. There is a marked identity about their features, person, manners and costume, so unmistakable that it betrays their nationality in a moment. Particular fashions and modes of dress give them no concern whatever. All their garments look as if they were made after the same pattern out of the same material and from the same piece of cloth. In short, one Chinaman looks almost exactly like another, but very unlike any body else.

Let us now place ourselves in front of one of these xanthous children of the flowery land and survey him somewhat minutely. His hat possesses a brim of enormous width, is manufactured out of ratan or bamboo splints and has an indentation made in the top expressly for the accommodation of his cue. He very seldom, however, wears this appendage tucked up in his hat, but generally allows it to trail about his back and legs as young girls sometimes do ribbons. This pig-tail he loves as he does his life and he would as willingly have his right arm amputated as part with it. It is his character—his badge of his respectability.

His coat, which is fashioned very much like a pea-jacket, is made of crow-colored cotton cloth of flimsy texture, and buttons loosely around him as low down as convenience will permit. His pantaloons, the legs of which are a trifle smaller than a medium-sized meal-bag, are composed of the same stuff as his coat and terminate at about the middle of his shins. His shoes or sandals—minus socks, for he never wears any—are hewn out of solid wood and taper towards the toe nearly to a sharp point.

As he moves along before us in these uncouth habiliments—his feet in rude wooden shoes, his legs bare, his breeches loosely flapping against his knees, his skirtless pea-jacket hanging in large folds around his waist, his broad-brimmed chapeau rocking on his head, and his cue sweeping about his back—I can compare him to nothing so appropriately as to a tadpole walking on stilts!

The few exceptions are the mandarins who robe themselves in long figured gowns and some of the wealthier classes who wear silk and satin goods instead of cotton fabrics. But the description given above will suit at least nine out of every ten.

According to the most reliable estimates there are at the present time about forty thousand Chinese in California and every vessel that arrives from the Celestial Empire brings additional immigrants. A few females are among the number and among these good morals are unknown. They have no regard whatever for chastity or virtue.

On holidays the *elite* braid their hair into a kind of crest which, as it is worn upon the head, bears a strong resemblance to the tuft of feathers upon the noddle of a peacock. Those who are from the extreme northern parts of the Chinese empire are the ugliest and most rugged featured human beings I ever saw.

What the majority of them do for a livelihood is more than I can tell, as they have but few visible occupations. The laundry business affords those who live in San Francisco the most steady employment and in passing their premises the eye is often attracted to such "Celestial" signs as "Kum Kee. Washer." and "Wong Cho. Washing and Ironing—$3 per Doz." Catching and drying fish is a business in which they engage but do not carry on extensively.

Here and there you will find one in a public house, filling the place of a cook or a waiter. But it goes desperately against the grain with them to take the situation of servants among white people as they are constitutionally haughty and conceited and believe themselves to be superior to us in all respects. So exalted an opinion have they of themselves that they think they are the most central, civilized and enlightened people on earth, and that they are the especial favorites of heaven. They look upon us and all other white-skinned nations as "outside barbarians," and think we are unduly presumptuous if we do not pay them homage! The majority of them lead a very inactive and unproductive life.

So sparing are they in their meals that it is seldom they eat any thing but boiled rice, and even this, which they bring with them from China, is very inferior to that raised in the Carolinas. It is an amusing spectacle to see one of them feeding on this grain. Holding a bowl of the rice in such a manner that the nearer edge of it almost touches his chin, and grasping two penholders between his fingers and thumb, he feeds himself with a lively and dexterous motion of the hand, not very unlike a musician playing upon a jewsharp. He continues the feast without intermission until he has finished eating. He seems to cram the food down his throat rather than let it undergo the usual process of mastication.

The Americans salute them all indiscriminately by the easy and euphonious appellation of "John," to which they reply as readily as if they were addressed by their true names. They return the compliment by applying the same term to us, equally indiscriminately. A great number of them think "John" is the only name white people have and if they have occasion to speak to an American or European woman, they call her "John," too!

They are deplorably addicted to wasting time in games of chance and there are a dozen and a half gambling houses in San Francisco under their especial control and direction.

Their money is chiefly composed of brass and copper coins, stamped with the characters of their alphabet. Hardened rice and stamped slices of pasteboard are also current among them as mediums of exchange.

Is this Chinese immigration desirable? I think not! In what capacity do they contribute to the advancement of American interests? Are they engaged in any thing that adds to the general wealth and importance of the country? Will they discard their clannish prepossessions, assimilate with us, buy of us, and respect us? Are they not so full of duplicity, prevarication and pagan prejudices, and so enervated and lazy that it is impossible for them to make true or estimable citizens?

Under the existing laws of our government, they, as well as all other foreigners, are permitted to work the mines in California as long as they please, and as much as they please without paying any thing for the privilege, except a small tax to the State.

The Chinese are more objectionable than other

foreigners because they refuse to have dealing or intercourse with us. Consequently there is no chance of making any thing of them either in the way of trade or labor. They are ready to take all they can get from us but are not willing to give any thing in return. They did not aid in the acquisition or settlement of California and they do not intend to make it their future home. They will not become permanent citizens nor identify their lives and interests with the country. They neither build nor buy, nor invest capital in any way that conduces to the advantage of any one but themselves. They have thousands of good-for-nothing gewgaws and worthless articles of *virtu* for sale, and our people are foolish enough to buy them.

Though they hold themselves aloof from us, contemn and disdain us, they have guaranteed to them the same privileges that we enjoy and are allowed to exhaust the mines that should be reserved for us and our posterity—that is if they are worth reserving at all. Their places could and should be filled with worthier immigrants—Europeans who would take the oath of allegiance to the country, work both for themselves and for the commonwealth, fraternize with us, and finally, become a part of us.

I cannot perceive what right these semi-barbarians have in California. Still they are received with a flattering welcome. They are taken by the hand with

"I have frequently seen Americans relinquish
the side-walk to them."

an obsequious grasp, as if their favor was earnestly desired.

Their mining implements and boots (the only articles of merchandise they purchase from us) are sold to them at even less rates than to our own countrymen, more from curiosity than from any other cause. For some unaccountable reason they are treated with a degree of deference and civility which is really surprising. To humor their arrogance and presumption, I have frequently seen Americans, in crowded places, relinquish the side-walk to them, and betake themselves to the middle of a rough and muddy street. Moreover, they are petted as if they were really what they preposterously fancy themselves—the most elevated and exalted of the human race.

However, they have neither the strength of body nor the power of mind to cope with us in the common affairs of life and our people will not always treat them with undue complaisance. They must work for themselves, or we will make them work for us. No inferior race of men can exist in these United States without becoming subordinate to the will of the Anglo-Americans. It was so with the negroes and the Indians and it will be so with the Chinese in California. The Indians, it is true, would not submit to be enslaved, but they had to suffer exile, hunger and death as a consequence of their intractability.

CHAPTER SIX

DESOLATION AND
DESPAIR

CALIFORNIA has features as distinct and peculiar as the Alps or the Andes. It cannot be mistaken for any other country; it is like no other region on the face of the earth. I speak of the country as I have seen it, not as a mere passing traveler but as an attentive observer. I emigrated to it as much in search of adventure as of profit. During the three years of my residence within its borders I have had ample opportunities to explore and scrutinize it as I desired. I am fully satisfied with my information upon this subject. I have seen all of it that is worth seeing, and a great deal besides. I crave no further knowledge of it than I now possess.

While there is any unoccupied land between the British boundaries of Maine and the Mexican limits of Texas, between the Florida Reefs and the Falls of St. Anthony, I would not advise any person to emigrate to California for the purpose of bettering his worldly condition. None of the land west of the Rocky Mountains has those elements of exuberant and permanent greatness so characteristic of the States east of the Rio Grande and the Mississippi. Oregon and Washington territories, Utah and New Mexico are tolerable countries, and superior to California, but owing to the general inferiority of their natural advantages, they can never become as powerful or important States as Louisiana or New York, Georgia or Illinois. The Pacific side of the continent is, as a general thing, far inferior to the Atlantic slope.

The present condition and future prospects of California actually portend much poverty and suffering. The very fact that thousands of men are working for nothing but their board, is of itself justifiable ground for this apprehension. More than a dozen stout, able-bodied men who asked nothing in compensation for their services but food, have applied to me for employment in a single day.

Many of the most menial and humiliating situations about hotels, stores and private residences are filled by these ill-fated men who, if they had the means, would be glad to shake off the dust of California from their feet. Misery and despair go to bed with them at night and if sickness overtake them, death is their remedy. Depressed in spirits and driven to desperation by bitter and repeated calamities, they take to the bottle for solace, or with bullet, knife, or poison, put an end to their wretched lives. Such is the history of many a man who has perished in this land of gold.

They left their homes flushed with hope, those dear to them imprinted the last kiss and bade them adieu with tearful eyes, but found consolation in the hope that they would soon return. The first letter home was received with ecstasy. For a few weeks all things promised well. Then, when no more letters came, fears began to be entertained. The unwelcome thought would occasionally flash through the mind that all was not well. Nor was it. Month after month slowly and gloomily passed away, without bringing any tidings of the poor deluded wanderers. It has now been so long since they were heard from that it is easier to reckon the time by years than by months.

All that can be concluded is that they lie some where within the confines of California, with no monument to reveal the place of their final slumber.

No country can ever become truly great unless it possesses abundant agricultural resources, and as California is deficient in this as well as in other respects, it is absurd to suppose that she will attract attention longer than her mines pay for working. The banks of the rivers and the localities in the San Jose, Sacramento, and San Joaquin valleys form exceptions to this general sterility. There the ground is low and moist or easily irrigated, the soil is extremely fertile and produces vegetables which, for size and powers of multiplication, have probably never been equaled. These spots, however, are little more, in comparison with the area of the State than are the roads of a county to the county itself. They cannot, therefore, be depended upon to supply the wants and necessities of the whole country should it ever be thickly settled throughout—an event which for the very reason I have mentioned above, I do not believe will ever take place.

As a few specimens of the vegetable monstrosities that have come under my notice, I may mention a beet that weighed forty-seven pounds, a thirty-two pound cabbage, a twenty-six pound turnip, a seven-pound Irish potato, and a sixty-four pound watermelon. Onions, lettuce, radishes, and other horticultural productions also grow to an enormous size.* Irish potatoes, however, are the most prolific crop that can be planted.

All of the arable parts of the State are now settled and farmers who go thither hereafter will either have to return or abandon altogether the idea of cultivating the soil for it will be impossible for them to make

---

* This has a direct bearing on the anecdote of the Floridian who ventured into a California fruiterer's shop. He hefted a vast green winter squash and enquired patronizingly: "Is this as big as your alligator pears grow hereabout?"

"Wherever do you come from, mister?" countered the Californian.

"Why, Florida, of course," replied the fellow.

"Wise guy," snapped the Californian. "Put down that grape!"

a subsistence out of the sterile hills of the upland.

That millions of dollars worth of gold have been taken from the mines, and that there is a vast amount still remaining, no one pretends to deny. But then it does not exist in the quantity that is generally supposed. There is nothing more uncertain as a business than gold mining in California.

Half the stories afloat concerning "wealthy returned Californians" are exaggerated beyond the power of tongue to describe. A young friend of mine who had been mining between two and three years started home with about one hundred and sixty dollars over and above his expenses. In speaking of his friends, I asked him what he was going to tell them when he got home. "Oh!" says he, "I won't admit that I have made so little, for if I do they'll accuse me of gambling and drinking or some other disreputable thing that I have never been guilty of. So I'll give out that I have made twelve or fifteen thousand dollars. About the time I have them all in a good humor I'll take an excursion down to New Orleans and thence to South America to seek my fortune." Thus, although he was honorable and not addicted to dissipation, he hadn't the nerve to tell the real truth.

This shows how easily these exaggerated rumors are set going. The further people live from California, the more credulous they are of golden legends, and I am persuaded that the young man above had no difficulty in making his neighbors in the East believe he was worth whatever amount he chose to tell them.

Extravagant as this story may sound it is not without a parallel. A man who had accumulated from three to four thousand dollars returned on a visit to his friends in the East. To test the credulity of the people, he put out the report that he had made five hundred thousand dollars. His story was received by the gaping neighbors without a doubt. At once our adventurer found himself the invited guest of nabobs who never knew him before he went to California though they had seen him hundreds of times.

I cannot close these remarks without offering a word of advice to the marriageable ladies. If you seek a rich husband, don't form a matrimonial alliance with an El Dorado Croesus for, in nine cases out of ten, a "wealthy Californian" is a poor man.

California will never become the land of promise which an enthusiastic imagination may picture. It is already a pandemonium, and it does not clearly appear how it can become an elysium.

The benefit of mines of the precious metals to the country in which they are found is still an open question. The weight of authority is against them and the history of Mexico and Peru cannot be quoted in their favor. Joseph Bonaparte remarked, "Gold is the sweat of the poor and the blood of the brave."

The concurrent testimony of all ages proves that

those nations who obtain their wealth by the indirect methods of agriculture, manufactures and commerce, are more happy and more prosperous than those who dig their treasures directly from the earth. The moral effect of sudden riches must also be taken into consideration. Few men can gaze undazzled at the splendor of a large fortune, and the more rapidly they acquire it, the more likely are they to grow dizzy in its contemplation.

We will not urge any complaint against the climate for all classes and conditions of men can be suited. Along the southern line of the State it is oppressively hot. In the north and among the mountains it is extremely cold. Snow to the depth of from two to ten feet is found there as late as August. Large quantities of this snow are brought down to the cities, a distance of more than two hundred miles, and sold as a substitute for ice.* In the middle or central parts of the State the climate is delightful and highly invigorating. Around San Francisco, during the winter season when it doesn't rain, the weather is unusually mild and pleasant. I have often heard it compared to the climate of Italy. It is not so agreeable in summer because the dust and winds prevail to such a degree through-

---

* An obvious parallel to the sybaritic practice, as recorded by Petronius, of the decadent Roman aristocracy who chilled their Falernian at bacchanalian orgies with snows imported by slave labor from the Apennines.

out the dry season as to become a source of extreme discomfort.

In San Francisco it is rarely ever too cold or too hot, though the weather frequently changes three or four times in a single day, from calm and warm to boisterous and cool, and from boisterous and cool to calm and warm again. In other places where the days are intolerably close and sultry it is necessary to have one or two blankets to sleep under at night. The remarkable aridity and unfruitfulness of the country at large may be ascribed to the protracted drought of the summer which begins in April and lasts until about the middle of November.

CHAPTER SEVEN

SUNDAY IN CALIFORNIA

THE Sabbath in California is kept, when kept at all, as a day of hilarity and bacchanalian sports rather than as a season of holy meditation or religious devotion. Horse-racing, cock-fighting, cony-hunting, card-playing, theatrical performances, and other elegant amusements are freely engaged in on this day.

It was about two months after my arrival in the land of gold and misery that I became acquainted with a renegade down-east Congregationalist preacher who invited me to accompany him on the following Sunday in a deer-chase. Throughout the country and in the mines, shooting-matches and bear-hunting afford pleasant pastimes. Gambling is also practiced to a considerable extent.

But we shall probably learn more of the manner in which Sunday is spent if we confine our attention to one of the larger cities; San Francisco, for example. Here regattas, duels and prize-fights are favorite diversions and the Lord's day seldom passes without witnessing one or the other.

Connected with a tippling-house on the corner of Washington and Montgomery streets, there is one of the finest billiard-saloons in the United States. It is very large and magnificently decorated, has twelve tables, and is furnished at a cost of twenty-five thousand dollars. To this place hundreds of infatuated men betake themselves every Sunday and it is an unusual thing, at any time, to find one of the tables unoccupied. Every day of the week, from breakfast time in the morning this saloon is thronged.* But the crowds are particularly large on Sunday because people have more leisure on that day.

What can we expect but an abuse of the Sabbath when we take into account the contrariety of characters, tastes, dispositions and religions here huddled together? When we scrutinize society we find that some of its members, the Chinese and other pagans, know nothing at all of our system or division of time and that they are, therefore, absolutely ignorant of the meaning of the word Sunday.

Masquerade balls, cotillion parties and jig dances fill up the list of Sunday diversions. On Pacific street

---

* Mr. Daniel Moriarity, a New York publican of widespread fame during the Prohibition era and well known to the editors, invariably opened his premises at six of a Sunday morning remarking that his most respectable custom derived from what he termed "the early church trade."

alone, the most notoriously profligate thoroughfare in the city, there are from twelve to fifteen dance-houses in which the terpsichorean art is practiced every night during the week, but usually with greater zest and animation on Sunday nights.

These fandangoes are principally under the super-intendence or management of Mexican girls. Although they engage in the lowest debaucheries throughout the week, they are strict attendants of the Catholic Church.

Before I ever saw any of the Mexican ladies I had heard the most glowing descriptions of their ravishing beauty. I must either discredit the accounts, or else conclude that my ideas of female beauty are very im-perfect. I have never yet beheld one of them who, according to my standard of good looks, was really beautiful. Their pumpkin hues and slovenly deport-ment could never awaken any admiration in me, even in California.

Bonnets among them are quite unknown. Half the time they go bare-headed through the streets and to church, just as they do about their homes. Most of them have a long, narrow shawl which is sometimes worn over the head as well as the shoulders. This shawl is an almost indispensable article of apparel, especially with the better classes who never appear in a public place, winter or summer, without it. They

wrap it around their face, head and shoulders so in-
geniously that spectators can not obtain a glimpse of
any part of their features save the forehead, eyes and
nose. The mouth, chin and cheeks are also concealed.

If they can only get one fine, fashionable garment
they think it makes amends for the bad material and
ill shape of all the others.* Nor are they particular to
have their whole person clothed at the same time. I
don't think I have ever seen one of them fully attired
in my life; something was always wanting. They may
be seen promenading the streets robed in the richest
silks that were ever woven in Chinese looms. But
when you gaze down at their lower extremities you
discover them stockingless, their feet thrust into a pair
of coarse slippers which expose to view a pair of rusty
heels that look as if no ablution had been performed
upon them for at least three moons.

The Mexicans, however, are fond of aquatic exer-
cises and they have several bathing establishments in
San Francisco for the accommodation of the public
(at one dollar per head for each bath!). It is a custom
with the proprietors when a gentleman retires to take
his bath, to dispatch a female servant to his room to
scour and scrub him off! As I resided near an Ameri-

---

* A circumstance which finds its almost precise counterpart
in the Western cow hand who, if his Stetson is sufficiently
handsome and costly, is sublimely indifferent to the remainder
of his attire.

"Since their arrival, there has been a gradual improvement of morals among the people."

can bath-house, I always patronized it in preference and did not acquaint myself with Mexican usages in this respect.

Lately, women of pure and lofty characters have emigrated to California and, since their arrival, there has been a gradual improvement of morals among the people. The Sabbath is now better observed than it used to be. Soon after their arrival, social circles were formed; refinement dawned upon a debauched and reckless community, decorum took the place of obscenity, kind and gentle words were heard to fall from the lips of those who before had been accustomed to taint every phrase with an oath.

Woman accomplished all this, and we should be ungrateful reprobates indeed if we did not honor, esteem and love her for it.

> "O, then,
> For wisdom's sake, a word that all men love;
> Or for love's sake, a word that loves all men;
> Or for men's sake, the authors of these women;
> Or for women's sake, by whom we men are men,
> Let us love women, and ourselves be true,
> Or else we harm ourselves, and wrong them too."

With the generous assistance and co-operation of the gentler sex, the various religious denominations have succeeded in establishing for themselves suitable places of worship in most of the cities and larger towns throughout the State. San Francisco now contains fourteen churches. The Swedenborgians, Universalists, Mormons, and sundry minor sects occasionally hold service in public halls and the Jews have two synagogues. There is also a pagan temple where the Chinese pay their adorations to Boodh, or to some other imaginary deity, whenever they experience a religious emotion.

CHAPTER EIGHT

SABBATH
SACRILEGE

IT WAS a beautiful Sabbath morning in November when the bells aroused me from a dreamy sleep. But before arising from my couch, being lazy and inclined to muse, I allowed my fancy to recall my departure from Carolina with all its attendant circumstances. The hour alone would have suggested such meditations for it was on a dewy morning that I bade farewell to the loved ones of my far-off home. I recalled the yellow lustre of the sun pouring his floods of golden light over the glistening tree-tops; the tender adieus, the streaming eyes, the murmured blessing. I remembered the sadness of my heart as I thought of the distance that would soon separate me from the friends and companions of my youth, and the high hopes which soothed my pain.

As I was thus pondering I heard the sound of drum, fife and clarionet, and stepping to the window to ascertain what was the meaning of this Sunday music echoing through the streets of San Francisco, I saw a tremendous grizzly bear, caged, and drawn by four spirited horses. Tacked to each side of the cage were large posters, which read as follows:—

FUN BREWING—GREAT ATTRACTION!
HARD FIGHTING TO BE DONE!
TWO BULLS AND ONE BEAR!

The citizens of San Francisco and vicinity are respectfully informed that at *four o'clock this afternoon, Sunday, Nov. 14th*, at *Mission Dolores, a rich treat* will be prepared for them, and that they will have an opportunity of enjoying a fund of the *raciest sport* of the season. TWO LARGE BULLS AND A BEAR, all in *prime condition for fighting*, and under the management of *experienced Mexicans*, will contribute to the *amusement of the audience*.

Programme—In two Acts.

Act I.

BULL AND BEAR—"HERCULES" and "TROJAN,"
Will be conducted into the arena, and there *chained together*, where they will fight *until one kills the other*.

JOSE IGNACIO, ⎱ Managers.
PICO GOMEZ, ⎰

Act II.

The great bull, "BEHEMOTH," will be *let loose in the arena*, where he will be *attacked by two of*

[94]

*the most celebrated and expert picadors of Mex-
ico*, and finally *dispatched after the true Spanish
method.*

Admittance $3—Tickets for sale at the door.

JOAQUIN VATRETO, ⎫
JESUS ALVAREZ, ⎬ Managers.
⎭

Mission Dolores, the place where these cruel sports
were to be held, is a small village about two miles
south-west of San Francisco which was first settled by
a couple of Roman Catholic priests during the American Revolution. The buildings are but one story in
height, covered with tiles, and are constructed of
adobe or sun-dried clay. The general aspect of the
place is distressingly shabby and gloomy. For scores
of years the inhabitants, who are a queer compound
of Spanish and Indian blood, have lived here in poverty, ignorance and inactivity.

But I am digressing. What was I to do about the
bull fight? I had never witnessed such an exhibition
and consequently had a great desire to see it. It was
Sunday, however, and how could I reconcile the instructions of a pious mother with an inclination so
much at variance with the divine command? Well,
without entering into any thing like a defence of my
determination, suffice it to say that I made up my mind
to go, and went. Anxious, however, to moderate or
diminish the sin as much as possible, I determined to

hear a sermon first and go to the bull-fight afterwards. For the sake of somewhat condensing the events of the day, I concluded to leave the city immediately and repair to the Mission, there to attend an antique Catholic church which has been built nearly three-quarters of a century.

Starting off with this view, I arrived within hearing of the priests' voices about the time they began to chant the service. On entering the rickety old church I learned that it was an extraordinary occasion with them and that a deal of unusual display might be expected. The rite or ceremony of high mass was to be performed. Monks and friars from the monasteries of Mexico were in attendance and the church was thronged with a large and heterogeneous crowd.

At four o'clock, the hour appointed for the fight between the bear and the bull, some popular airs were played by the musicians announcing that the amphitheatre, which fronted the church and stood but a few yards from it, was open for the reception of those who desired admission. I made my way to the ticket-office and handed three dollars to the collector. I found myself among the first who entered and as it was some time before the whole audience assembled, I had ample opportunities to scan the characters who composed it and to examine the arrangement and disposition of things around me.

The seats were very properly elevated so high above

the arena that no danger was likely to result from the furious animals, and I suppose five thousand persons could have been conveniently accommodated though only about three-fourths of that number were present.

Among the auditory I noticed many Spanish maids and matrons, who manifested as much enthusiasm and delight in anticipation of what was to follow as the most enthusiastic sportsman. Crying children in the arms of self-satisfied and admiring mothers, were there full of noise and mischief, and a nuisance as they always are in theatres and churches.

Of men, there were all sizes, colors and classes, such as California and California alone can bring together. There was one, however, who attracted my particular attention on this occasion. He sat a few feet from me on my left and the expression of his countenance was neither intellectual nor amiable. His acquirements and attainments were doubtless limited for he demeaned himself rudely and exhibited but little dignity of manner. It was a strange metamorphosis he had undergone since the morning. Only four hours had elapsed since I saw him officiating at the altar and feasting upon a substance which he believed to be the actual flesh and blood of Jesus Christ. In the forenoon of the Lord's day, he took upon himself the character of God's vicegerent, invested himself with sacerdotal robes, assumed a sanctified visage and discharged the sacred duties of his office. In the afternoon of the same

"There was one, however, who attracted my particular
attention on this occasion."

Sabbath he sanctioned merciless diversions, mingled on terms of equality with gamblers and desperados and held himself in readiness to exclaim Bravo! at the finale of a bull-fight.

By this time the whooping, shouting and stamping of the spectators attested that they were eager and restless to behold the brutal combat. An overture by a full brass band which had been chartered for the occasion, gave them assurance that their wishes would soon be complied with.

The music ceased, the trap-door of the bull's cage was raised and "Hercules," huge, brawny and wild, leaped into the center of the inclosed arena. His eyes glistened with defiance and he seemed to crave nothing so much as an enemy upon which he might wreak his vengeance. Just then two picadors—Mexicans on horseback—entered the arena with lassos in hand. Taurus welcomed them with an attitude of attack. He was about to rush upon one of their horses with the force of a battering-ram, when, with most commendable dexterity, the picador farthest off lassoed him by the horns and foiled him in his mad design. As quick as thought the horseman from whom the bull's attention had been diverted, threw his lasso around his horns also. In this way they brought him to a stand midway between them. A third person, a footman, now ran in, and seizing the bull's tail, twisted it until he fell flat on his side. Then by the help of an assistant, the end of a long log-chain was fastened to his right hind-leg. In this prostrated condition he was kept until the other end of the chain was secured to the left fore-leg of the bear.

Running a pair of large clasping-tongs under Bruin's trap-door, which was lifted just enough for the purpose, they grasped his foot, pulled it out and held it firmly while one of the party bound the opposite end of the chain fast to his leg with thongs. This done, they hoisted the trap-door sufficiently high to admit of his egress. Out stalked "Trojan," apparently too proud and disdainful to vouchsafe a glance upon surrounding objects. He was the largest grizzly bear I had ever seen.

The bull, now on his feet, needed no challenge. He was, if possible, more impetuous than the bear and didn't lose any time to measure the length of the chain. With unabated fierceness he darted at the bear, and struck him with an impetus that seemed to have been borrowed from Jove's own thunderbolt. As he came in contact with the bear, that amiable animal grappled him by the neck and squeezed him so hard that he could scarcely save himself from suffocation. The bull now found himself in a decidedly uncomfortable situation. Powerful as he was, he couldn't break loose from Bruin.

It was a stirring sight to see these infuriated and muscular antagonists struggling to take each other's life. It was enough to make a heathen generalissimo shudder to look at them, but the heartless Spanish ladies laughed, cheered, encored, clapped their hands, and waved their handkerchiefs.

Hercules quaked under the torturing hugs of Trojan. Trojan howled under the violent and painful perforation of Hercules. But the bear didn't rely alone on his arms. His massive jaws and formidable teeth were brought into service and he inflicted deep wounds in his rival's flesh. He seized the bull between the ears and nostrils and crushed the bones with such force that we could distinctly hear them crack! Nor were the stunning butts of the bull his only means of defence. His horns had been sharpened expressly for the occasion and he lacerated the bear most frightfully. It was a mighty contest—a desperate struggle for victory!

Finally, however, fatigued, exhausted, writhing with pain and weltering in sweat and gore, the bull shattered the lower jaw of the bear, and we could see the shivered bones dangling from their bloody recesses! Oh, heaven! what a horrible sight. How the blood curdled in my veins. Pish! what a timid fellow I am, to allow myself to be agitated. Shall I tremble at what the ladies applaud? Forbid it, Mars!

But, to wind up this part of our story, neither the bear nor the bull could stand any longer—their strength had completely failed and they dropped upon the earth, gasping as if in the last agony. While in this helpless condition the chain was removed from their feet, horses were hitched to them, and they were dragged from the arena to end their miseries in death.

The second act of the afternoon's entertainment was now to be performed. It would be unnecessary and painful to the feelings of the sensitive readers to dwell upon this murderous sport. It was a mere repetition, in another form, of the disgusting horrors of that which preceded it. Fully satiated with the barbarities I had already witnessed, I was further revolted by the peculiar sensations which the cognomen of one of the actors awakened within me. By reference to the advertisement it will be perceived that the two managers of this part of the proceedings were Joaquin Vatreto and Jesus Alvarez. The latter name sounded strangely in my ears. It occurred to me that it was peculiarly out of place in its present connection. What! Jesus at a bull-fight on Sunday, and not only at it, but one of the prime movers and abettors in it!

CHAPTER NINE

SACRAMENTO

SACRAMENTO is situated on the river and in the heart of the valley of the same name about one hundred miles north-east of San Francisco. It is the second city in the State in size, population and commerce, and contains from eight to ten thousand inhabitants—being nearly one fourth as large as San Francisco. It bears to San Francisco much the same relation that Columbia does to Charleston, or Albany to New York. From two to six steamboats daily ply between the two cities, conveying passengers and merchandise.

The banks of the river are very low and the current moves sluggishly towards the ocean. Flood-tide ascends almost as high as this place. The country for twenty-five miles on either side of the river is an unbroken plain, level as a floor. It would be invaluable for agricultural purposes were it not for the great freshets of the winter and spring and the incessant drought of the summer and fall—two serious disadvantages to the farmer. Sometimes the whole valley is completely overflowed and remains under water for two or three consecutive months. On these occasions it presents the appearance of a vast lake.

Many new immigrants who are ignorant of the freaks of California seasons arrive here in the summer and settle in this valley, thanking their stars that they were guided to a plat of so much promise. But when winter comes and the windows of heaven are opened, the river rises and the cattle are drowned, the houses swept off and the settlers are compelled to fly to the upland to save their lives. Then they begin to discover the gloomy fact that they have been caught in a snare.

The site of the city, so smooth and flat, would be one of the most beautiful in the world but for the lack of sufficient elevation. For the first two or three years after its settlement the inhabitants did nothing to protect it from the floods, but afterwards, becoming tired of navigating the streets in scows and skiffs and willing to retain some of their goods and chattels about their premises, they built a temporary levee which has since kept them tolerably dry.

At present the legislature meets in this place but that august body is possessed of a remarkably roving disposition, having held its sessions at four different places within the last four years at an extra expense to the State of nearly two hundred thousand dollars.

There is no capitol or statehouse, nor is it likely that California will ever be able to build one while its finances are so recklessly managed. The receipts and expenditures of the State have, from the organization of its government to the present time, been intrusted to men who, to say nothing of their dishonesty, were as ignorant of the uses of money as a prodigal minor. Consequently they have entailed a public debt upon the people of more than three millions of dollars without effecting any general improvements excepting a marine hospital. This distinguished body, which now holds its deliberations in the court-house, contains some of the most precious scamps that ever paid devotion to the god of pelf. I have no wish to deal in personalities but I could here mention names which are notoriously infamous all over the Atlantic States.

Are such men fit to enact laws for the commonwealth? However, they are the only class of persons who are intrusted with the functions of legislation in this abominable land of concentrated rascality. The people of California would as soon elect an honest, upright man to office as Italian banditti would choose a moralist for their captain. No one here can be successful unless he assimilates himself to the people. He must carouse with villains, attend Sunday horse-races and bull-fights and adapt himself to every species of depravity and dissipation.

Thus must a man discipline himself before he can receive the support and patronage of the public. It matters not what his occupation may be, whether mer-

"No one here can be successful unless he
assimilates himself to the people."

chant, mechanic, lawyer or doctor, he is sure to be ostracized if he stands aloof from the vices and follies of the populace. Of course there are a few exceptions. Some men, thank heaven, have an innate abhorrence of every thing that savors of meanness or vulgarity, and they have nerve enough to cling to their principles at all times and in all places. They have clearly defined ideas of right and wrong and regulate their lives and conduct accordingly. But there are few such men in California! They are discountenanced, neglected, sneered at, and flouted with opprobrious epithets. They are in bad odor; the majority is against them.

The scoundrels are in power and they have wrecked the country. Today the State is lawless, penniless and powerless. Such is the effect of the union of two bad things—a bad people and a bad country.

The common interests have been confided to political charlatans whose actions in every instance have been detrimental to the interests of the country. As a poor client suffers in the hands of a pettifogger, or as a patient laboring under an obscure and dangerous disease sinks under the treatment of a quack, so has this poor, sick California suffered and sunk through the agency of her knavish managers.

Leaving these wire-pulling senators and hireling assemblymen, let us take a short stroll through one or two of the principal streets. We shall not observe any thing either curious or commendable in the styles of architecture. The houses are low, rarely exceeding two stories in height, and are built mostly of wood in the very cheapest manner. All the lumber used in their construction was brought from Oregon.

Here and there stands a plain but uncommonly stout and substantial brick store. I have never seen any buildings in the Atlantic States equal, in durability and security against fire, to the brick structures in California. They must build them so for reasons heretofore given. Stone is not used at all; there is none in the vicinity.

As we wend our way through the town, we pass dozens of miserable, filthy little hotels, in any of which we can procure a bad meal for a dollar. A palatable dinner in one of the more respectable hotels will cost us twice that amount. We shall be considerably amused at the queer and unique canvas signs nailed over the doors of some of the dirty little huts and shanties around us. One of the taverns announces that it has "Tip-top Accommodations for Man and Beast," at another we can find "Good Fare, and Plenty of it," a third promises "Rest for the Weary and Storage for Trunks," a fourth invites us to "Come in the Inn, and take a Bite." A fifth informs us that "Eating is done here," a sixth assures us that "We have Rich Viands and Mellow Drinks," while a seventh admonishes us to "Replenish the Stomach in our House."

A bar, at which all kinds of liquors are dealt out, is attached to each of these establishments. It is generally a greater source of profit to the proprietor than the table. Small straw cots with coarse blankets which have never been submitted to any cleansing process, are provided for the guests to sleep on. When the guests retire they seldom remove any of their clothes except their coats, and sometimes not even those. In the morning when they rise to perform their ablutions, a single wash-pan answers for all, and one towel, redolent of a week's wiping, serves every guest.*

Most of the population of the northern part of the State lay in their supplies of provisions, clothing and mining implements in Sacramento. We shall notice several teams and pack-trains in the streets, loading and preparing to start on their journey. Mules and oxen are chiefly used, though for hauling short distances over good roads, horses are employed.

Some of the more remote mining districts are so rugged and mountainous that it is impossible to reach them with wagons or other vehicles and the only means of transporting merchandise is upon the backs of mules. These hybrids, unamiable as is their appearance, are truly valuable for this purpose. They carry ponderous burdens, walk with ease upon the brink of

---

* A commentary on this unwholesome circumstance would seem to be furnished by a state regulation prohibiting the maintainance and use of the unsanitary roller towel in New York.

a precipice, and can be kept in good serviceable condition by provender on which a horse would starve. After making a few trips they become very tractable and it requires only four or five men to manage fifty or sixty of them. They do not go abreast, but each follows closely behind another, Indian fashion, and they will travel patiently in this way from morning till night, rarely ever attempting a stampede.

Between the petty merchants who sell goods to those teamsters and muleteers, there is great rivalry and competition. I call them petty merchants because there are so many more of them than the business justifies or demands that they have to resort to the most contemptible devices to pay current expenses. Indeed I don't believe half of them earn their support. The reader may think this strange, and wonder why men continue in an occupation which doesn't yield them a maintenance. They do not continue in it; their losses soon compel them to leave. But the departure of one victim only opens the way for the arrival of another.* Their stands are immediately occupied by novices who, after the lapse of a few

---

* This prudent habit of getting out of one's business effectively prevented a large number of California merchants from becoming engulfed in the even more disastrous bankruptcies which must accompany the three-billion-dollar volume of trade per annum now recorded in the Bay Area of San Francisco alone.

months, sink under the same fate that overwhelmed their luckless predecessors.

Such is the routine of affairs all over the State. I have never known the time here when business was not clogged with double the number of traders it required. Ever since San Francisco and Sacramento were founded they have been overwhelmed with merchants, and this has been the case with every other city and town of any note throughout the State. In commercial circles you hear continual complaints of the dullness of the times. The merchants are always grumbling because they have nothing to do and wondering when their business will improve. They live on the airy diet of hope. As soon as one simpleton sacrifices his effects and retires a sadder and a wiser man, another fool steps in and takes his place.

Question the New York, Baltimore and Boston shippers concerning the results of their ventures, and they will tell a doleful story. Now and then, it is true, when the markets are low, as they sometimes are, a shipment turns out lucrative beyond anticipation, but one gainful shipment occasions scores of unprofitable ones. Dependent as the State is upon importations for all that she consumes, it must be expected that the markets will be very fluctuating and changeable. The price of any article does not remain the same two weeks at a time.

There is almost always a superfluity of merchandise in market. Yet, by the time this merchandise falls into the hands of the actual consumer, it usually costs him from one to four hundred per cent more than he would have to pay for it in the Atlantic States. The consignee will probably sell it to a speculator—the speculator to a wholesale merchant—the wholesale merchant to a jobber—the jobber to a retailer—the retailer to a muleteer, and the muleteer to the final purchaser or consumer. Thus the charges accruing on it after its arrival, render it very costly.

Instances of the perfidy and dishonesty of California merchants would be like taking inventory of blades of grass in a meadow. A New Yorker consigned twenty thousand dollars worth of merchandise to two different commission houses (ten thousand to each), with limited instructions—that is, not to sell for less than a certain sum. The factors received the goods, hurried them through the market, put the funds in their pockets, and wrote to the consignor informing him that his ventures had been consumed by fire, and sympathizing with him in his losses!

A whole cargo of wares and merchandise valued at a trifle less than three hundred thousand dollars was intrusted to another man who disposed of it and absconded with the money. Volumes upon volumes might be filled with accounts of the crimes and shortcomings of this wretched country.

If, reader, you would know California, you must go live there. It is impossible for me to give, or for you to receive a correct impression of it on paper,—like Thomas, the unbelieving disciple, you must *see* and *feel* before you can be convinced.

On the night of the 2d of November, Sacramento was almost entirely destroyed by fire. Twenty-two hundred buildings, with other property, valued at ten millions of dollars, were completely reduced to ashes. Men, women and children ran to and fro in the greatest confusion, excited almost to frenzy in the effort to save their lives and effects. Within six hours after the fire first broke out, more than nine-tenths of the city were swept into oblivion and the people were left to sleep on the naked earth without any shelter but the clothing they had on.

Provisions at the time were scarcer than I ever knew them before, and the extraordinarily high prices which they commanded almost precluded the poorer classes from buying or using them at all. Flour sold at forty-two dollars per barrel, pork at fifty-five, and other eatables in about the same ratio. Farther in the interior the times were still harder. In some of the distant mining localities flour sold as high as three dollars per pound—equal to five hundred and eighty-eight dollars per barrel, and I have seen children crying to their parents for bread, when there was none to give them.

A California conflagration is a scene of the most

awful grandeur that the mind is capable of conceiving. When fire is once communicated to the buildings, especially if it be in the dry season, it doesn't smoulder, but blazing high in the air, and spreading far and wide, it consumes every thing within its reach. It leaves nothing behind but cinders and desolation. No one of the present day, out of California, has ever seen such pyramids of flame.

Before taking our final leave of Sacramento, we mustn't fail to get a glimpse of the Three Cent Philosopher, a Mormon polygamist who is an extortionate usurer. He was born in the State of New York near the hallowed spot where Jo Smith received his apostolic diploma. The Three Cent Philosopher is the wealthiest man in Sacramento, and is as tenacious of his property as of his life. It is supposed that he is worth very near half a million dollars.

Though he believes in polygamy and practices it, he never lives with more than one spouse at a time; to have them all around him at once would be too expensive. When he travels on a steamboat he always takes deck passage and carries food in his pockets to avoid the extra expense of dining at the table. While passing through the streets he keeps a vigilant lookout for stray nails, old horse-shoes, pieces of bagging and other refuse, which he picks up and lugs home.

His disposition is quite as sweet as wormwood, and his household is usually a scene of as much calm and

domestic bliss as a family of tomcats. He is in the habit
of bickering with his family at least once every day,
and when he does so he rouses the whole neighborhood with the noise of his oaths and imprecations.

He is at enmity with all the world and is despised
by everybody. If his neighbor looks at him, he curses
him, and if an acquaintance says good-morning to him,
he tells him to go to h-ll. He has never been known to
speak a good word concerning his nearest relations.
To sum up all, he is the extract of ill-breeding, the
essence of vulgarity, and the quintessence of meanness.

CHAPTER TEN

STOCKTON AND
SONORA

I HAVE perambulated the streets of San Francisco, Sacramento, Marysville and Stockton. But of all the California cities, after San Francisco, Stockton is my choice. It is named in honor of Commodore R. F. Stockton and is situated on a tributary of the San Joaquin river which eventually empties into the Bay of San Francisco. Being but a little over one hundred miles to the east of San Francisco, it enjoys the advantages of daily steamboat communication. Owing to the narrow banks of the stream and the shallowness of the water, the vessels are much smaller than those employed upon the Sacramento. It contains from six to seven thousand inhabitants. Though only the fourth city in the State in population, it is the third in business. All the residents of the southern mines draw their supplies from Stockton, and as it is blessed with a mild climate, it is frequently resorted to by those who seek pastime or recreation.

The San Joaquin valley, in the midst of which this

city is situated, would probably be the best agricultural land in the State if the water could be drained from it, but in its present low and boggy condition it is utterly unfit for cultivation. It takes its name from the low-banked river which meanders through it, and is as level as a garden. No vegetable production is found upon it, except the tule, a tall, pithy species of rush.

This valley affords another evidence of the unfavorable condition of the country. It shows conclusively that even the most valuable parts of the State are encumbered with insurmountable impediments. The bottom lands, which are mainly relied upon for agricultural purposes, are too wet to till, and too low to drain. The uplands are so dry and sterile that neither grains, plants nor fruits can be raised upon them. There is either too much moisture or none at all. It is a land of mountains and mud-holes.

It is very probable, however, that in the progress of time as the other members of the confederacy become burdened with population, the more eligible parts of this State will be settled and by means of irrigation made tolerably productive. But when California is thus peopled and converted into a place of permanent habitation, it will not be by any attractions it can offer to immigrants. They may make it their home as a dernier resort, but they will not do it as a matter of choice. So long as there is any unappropriated territory in other parts of the Union, California will not be in demand.

We shall find but few things deserving attention in the city of Stockton, having already examined its archetypes, San Francisco and Sacramento. It is due to this place to remark that, notwithstanding all its Peter Funk and Cheap John establishments, it sustains a better character than any other city in the State. Though it has its share of groggeries and gambling-houses, and is in most respects fitted out in true California style, it is not infested with so many drones and desperadoes as are usually met with in neighboring towns. I am well acquainted with many of its citizens and I know them to be estimable men—not too lazy to work, nor too sour to laugh at a merry thing.

Sonora is an inland town situated in the midst of one of the richest mineral regions in the southern part of the State. From Stockton a stage affords the most convenient and expeditious means of reaching this place, which lies about fifty miles to the south-east. Starting early in the morning, we travel as fast as a dare-devil driver can make four horses convey us. A part of the country over which our road leads us is an elevated plain. Entirely destitute of trees and other vegetable products, it presents a most dreary and uninviting prospect. We see nothing around us but the naked earth. There is no accommodation for either bird or beast—no resting-place for the one, nor food for the other.

About twelve o'clock we came to the Stanislaus River, a small tributary stream of the San Joaquin. Here we stop to change horses and get dinner, there being a sort of bastard hotel near the brink of the river. Numerous Indians, naked and hungry, could be seen prowling about this place, or seated in squads partaking of a mess of worms, young wasps, grasshoppers, or any other similar dainty to which their good stars may lead them. They have now given up open hostility and are comparatively peaceable. But they still secretly cherish the most implacable enmity to our race and improve every opportunity to dispatch us when they can do so without being detected. Our people, however, retaliate by deliberately shooting them down whenever they come in their way with as much nonchalance as though they were squirrels.

Having appeased our appetites and secured the services of a fresh team, we cross the river and resume our journey. As we advance towards the place of our destination the face of the country changes from level plains to rugged slopes and woodlands. Now it winds over rocky glades, hills and gullies and we are jarred and shaken without mercy, but being in charge of a very skillful driver, we are drawn safely over every rock and crag.

"We repair to the best hotel in the place."

Arriving in Sonora between sundown and dark, we repair to the best hotel in the place, a one-story structure built of unhewn saplings, covered with canvas and floored with dirt. It consists of one undivided room in which the tables, berths and benches are all arranged. Here we sleep, eat and drink. Four or five tiers of berths or bunks, one directly above another, are built against the walls.

The bedding is composed of a small straw mattress about two feet wide, an uncased pillow stuffed with the same material, and a single blanket. When we creep into one of these nests it is optional with us whether we unboot or uncoat ourselves, but it would be looked upon as an act of ill-breeding, even in California, to go to bed with one's hat on. Having once resigned ourselves to the arms of Morpheus, we are not likely to be disturbed by the drunken yells and vociferations of night-brawlers, now that we have become accustomed to such things. The noisy curses of the rabble will have no more effect upon us than the roaring waterfall or the mill-wheel has upon the miller.

Night glides away, morning dawns, and we rise from our bunks to battle with another day. On the outside of the tavern, whither we betake ourselves to wash, are a tub of water, a basin and a towel for all the guests. But as only one person can perform his ablutions at a time, it will be necessary for us to form ourselves in a line and take our turn—the first comers being entitled to the front places.

We are now ready to replenish the inner man. The bar is convenient for those who wish to imbibe. Breakfast is announced. We seat ourselves at the table. Before us is a reasonable quantity of beans, pork and flapjacks served up in tin plates. Pea tea, which the landlord calls coffee with a bold emphasis, is handed to us. We help ourselves to such other things as may be within reach. Neither spices, sauces nor seasonings are necessary to accommodate them to the palate. Our appetites need no nursing. Honest hunger disdains such dyspeptic accompaniments as the contents of cruets and casters. The richest condiments are the poorest provisions.

Our fast is broken—we are satisfied. The proprietor of the hotel, with his two male assistants, begins to clear off the table. Women have no hand in these domestic affairs. There is not a female about the establishment.* All the guests, owners and employees are men. The dishes are washed and the blankets are straightened in the berths.

While the cook is preparing dinner some of the tavern-loungers seat themselves around the table to take a friendly game of whist, seven-up, laugh-and-lay-down, old-maid, commerce or matrimony. Others saunter off to the gambling houses, of which there are

* We hear differently.

[122]

about half a dozen in the place, to play at roulette, monte, faro, poker, twenty-one, all-fours or lansquenet. Such is hotel life in California, especially in the country towns and throughout the mining region.

Frequently many of the guests are fuddled, and as there are no partitions or apartments in the building by which one person or set of persons may be separated from another, they are a most prolific source of annoyance to their sober neighbors. I recollect one occasion particularly, when, fatigued by a long day's journey, I stopped at one of these mountain taverns in the hope of enjoying a comfortable night's rest. Soon after eating my supper, which consisted of the standard dish of pork and beans, I crept into one of the farthest bunks. Although annoyed by the blackguardism and segar fumes of a group of drunken cardplayers who occupied a table near the centre of the room, these noisy swaggering inebriates did not prevent me from sleeping. I had become habituated to witnessing such nocturnal carousals.

Towards midnight in came a wild, blustering lunatic who had lost his reason about a week before, yelling and screaming as if a legion of fiends were after him. He was bare-footed, bare-headed and bare-legged, having no clothing upon his person except a shirt.

I understood afterwards that he had been roaming about the place four or five days and nights in this condition. Making some inquiry concerning his history, I learned that he was a lawyer by profession and that he had formerly figured as an able and influential member of the Maine Legislature.

Shortly after his arrival here, not finding employment for his talent as a counselor, he determined to seek the favor of the mines, but his efforts in that quarter proved unavailing. For nearly a year he had toiled vigorously and incessantly, but to no purpose. Disappointed and chagrined at the result he resigned himself to the bottle. The remembrance of his dependent and distant family, coupled with the mischievous influence of ardent spirits, increased and sharpened his mental suffering. His reason lost its equilibrium, and we now find him a raving maniac. More than half naked, friendless and forlorn, he wanders about the streets and through the woods, day and night—a poor, miserable, crazy vagabond.

Why, it may be asked, was there no public provision made for the removal and security of this pitiable nuisance? Simply because it was in California. Here, where there is nothing as it should be, this unhappy man was allowed to run at large. No one cared for him. He was supposed to be harmless and was therefore permitted to live. If he had inflicted any bodily injury upon any one he would probably have been shot or stabbed, and that would have been the end of the drama. Cases of this or a similar character are to be met with almost every day. I only mention this as a single instance.

To give a faint idea of the precocity and waywardness of youth in this country, I will relate a bloody incident which occurred at another hotel where I had put up for a night's lodging. In this case the landlord, a short, lean Massachusetts Yankee, was married and had his family with him. His eldest son, Ned, had not seen his ninth year. Nevertheless, this boy had learned to gamble and it was very evident that his parents cared very little about the matter. They even permitted him to play cards in their own house and seemed to pride themselves upon his proficiency.

I watched Little Ned more than an hour. He handled the cards with so much grace, skill and agility, and seemed to be so perfectly familiar with every branch of the game, that I could not withhold my admiration. It may be questioned whether Hoyle himself was so conversant with diamonds, hearts, clubs and spades at so early an age.

As the night advanced, the parties became involved in a quarrel. Some one accused Ned of unfairness. Violent oaths and maledictions followed this accusation. Inflamed with anger, and assuming a menacing attitude, Ned denounced his accuser (a full grown man, three times as large and four times as old as himself,) as "a pusillanimous liar and scoundrel," and added, "G—d d—n you, I'll shoot you!" By this time the excitement had reached a high pitch.

Things began to wear an alarming aspect. Several persons took sides in the matter, some for Ned and some against him. Ned's friends took upon themselves a war of loud invectives and imprecations. The bandying of gross epithets attracted the attention of a large crowd.

The occasion was pregnant with mischief. One of the desperadoes jerked a bowie knife from his pocket and was about to plunge it into the body of his antagonist, when another drew a revolver and shot him. A few struggles—a few groans, and the fallen man had ceased to live.

But the injury was not confined to him alone. As the ball passed through the breast of the man at whom it was aimed, it lodged in the shoulder of an innocent spectator.

And now was enacted one of those awful scenes of retribution for which California is so notorious. The man who had just committed the homicide was seized by the mob and amid loud cries of "hang him! hang him!" led out to a tree and there summarily executed according to the prompt sentence of the excited multitude. It was a season of dreadful uproar and commotion. The man who was shot had not been dead half an hour before his murderer was suspended by the neck between heaven and earth.

Thus we have seen the blood of two men shed in the quarrel of a stripling who had not attained half the age of manhood, but who already was a reckless and abandoned little gambler. If we deemed it necessary we might cite other instances of a similar character. Suffice it to say that this boy, Ned, may be taken as a fair sample of the rising generation in California.

The same unlimited freedom is extended to them all; they are allowed to do just as they please. Is it to be supposed that parents who put no restraint upon themselves will govern their children with propriety? If the father is an habitual gambler, drunkard and desperado, will not the son be so too?

The truth is, there is no attention paid to the moral, mental or physical discipline of youth in this country. They are left to their own will and inclination to grow up like the plants and weeds in a neglected garden, without culture or training. Surrounded as they are with so many examples of depravity, what sort of men and women are they likely to be?

It is probable that the world has never reared such a horde of accomplished scamps and vagabonds, male and female, as will soon emerge from the adolescent population of the Eureka State. The signs of the times warrant this conclusion. How can it be otherwise when they are familiar with every vice and strangers to every virtue? It matters not how strict or careful the parents themselves may be, it is impossible for them to shield their children from the baneful influences of the neighborhood.

A man might as well think of raising a healthy and stalwart family in the midst of a malarious swamp as to think of rearing decent sons and daughters in California.

A few words now in regard to this town of Sonora. It is built upon the slope of a long hill, and contains about four thousand inhabitants. Only one street traverses it. Unlike most other towns, its length is very much disproportioned to its breadth. The town is over a mile long and only about one hundred yards wide, so that the single street which passes through it affords an ample avenue for the intercourse and business operations of the people. The houses, or, more properly speaking, the shanties, are built close together and open on the street in city style. Indeed it is here called a city, and is governed by a mayor and common council.

In fact every collection of houses in this country, every hamlet, every village, every town, is called a city. No matter if there be only half a dozen houses in a place it is termed a city, always taking the name of the locality upon which it is built, as Collusi city, Stanislaus city, Marin city. I have visited two or three of these California "cities" that contained but a couple of frail tenements each and four or five old bachelor inhabitants.

It is in this neighborhood that a wonderful deal of finesse is practiced by a set of land-speculators. Scattering themselves over the country, they lay claim to certain eligible plats which they then allege Nature has formed expressly for capitals and queen cities. Large maps, margined with laudatory remarks and setting forth the peerless advantages of this point and that, are committed to oily-tongued agents for general circulation. The people are informed that such a place was destined to become a metropolis. All the surrounding mountains, hills, valleys and plains are bound to become tributary to it and the great system and machinery of the world can't move on harmoniously without it.

Those who secured the first choice of lots would at once be in possession of a lordly fortune. This, as a matter of course, is all sheer humbug. Nevertheless, in California, where humbug mingles with every transaction of life, and where people are ever ready to lay hold of any scheme that promises money, it has the desired effect.

Many persons had confidence in these projects, and made investments in them. Besides several individual cases of which I might speak, I am acquainted with a company of men who laid out more than one hundred and fifty thousand dollars in this questionable

[129]

species of property. Today their investment is not worth two cents.

It was perfectly amusing sometimes to witness the working of these bastard enterprises. The authors and agents of the plan, having their topographic charts and every thing in readiness, would bustle about among the people, pointing out and explaining the favorable and commanding situation of the place, assuring them that the attention of the whole country was directed to it, and giving the most exaggerated accounts of the demand for lots. In this way they would soon get up a great excitement, (it requires but a small matter to excite the people in California).

In a few instances as many as seventy or eighty persons have been known to purchase interests in one of these bubble cities. Three weeks afterwards, there would probably be only one or two men on the ground and no marks or vestiges of a city, except, perhaps, a few deserted cloth tents. It must be admitted that the projectors of these ephemeral cities made money.

I know several Germans, who, though proverbially cautious in the matter of dollars and cents, bought four lots for thirteen thousand dollars, which they afterwards offered to me at ninety-five percent discount! I wouldn't have taken the whole or any part of the plot at any price.

I have alluded to the excitability of the Californians.

This is a remarkable trait in their character. The least thing of unusual occurrence fires their fancy and sets them in motion. If a terrier catches a rat or if a big turnip is brought to market, the people cluster together and scramble for a sight with as much eagerness and impetuosity as a party of children would scramble after a handful of sweetmeats.

If, in these hasty gatherings, one man happens to tread on the toes of another, it only requires one minute for the injured party to shoot the offender, two minutes for some body else to stab the shooter, and three minutes for the whole crowd to hang the stabber.

While in and about Sonora, we have an opportunity of inspecting all the various systems of mining that are carried on in California. The whole earth, for some distance around, is literally turned upside down or inside out. On the left they are using the common single-hand rocker. On the right, sluicing, and in another place, sinking deep shafts. We shall here find a great many Mexican miners who make deep pits and excavations in the hills, and who are generally very successful in their operations. Sometimes they will go forty or fifty feet into the earth without finding an atom of the precious metal, but it is very seldom that they mistake their ground.

Except in working quartz veins, machinery has been but little employed in developing the mineral resources of the State. I am inclined to the opinion that it might be advantageously applied in gathering the gold in whatever form it may exist.

A part of the preceding chapter was devoted to observations upon the habits of life and personal appearance of the miner, but I neglected to mention the long hair upon his head and face. He neither shaves nor shears and so has no use for either razors or scissors. The tonsorial art is, in his estimation, a most reprehensible and unmanly innovation. Looking upon it as one of the fashionable foibles of society, he disavows all connection with it. He believes that Nature is not apt to make mistakes, that all things were created about right. Furthermore, he believes that hair was placed upon man's head and face to harmonize with the other organs of his body, and that if it is cut, the whole animal economy will be more or less enervated.

I confess myself, in fact, a convert to his notions. To say that the whiskers or the hair should never be trimmed would be as much as to say that the finger-nails should never be pared. While to say that the beard or the hair should be cut close to the skin would be the same as saying that the finger-nails should be pulled out by the roots. If we shave the chin and the cheeks, why not the head, the hands and the arms? How comes it that hair is less tolerable on the side of the face than on the back of the hand?

The Chinaman shaves his head all over except a small

"What would we think of the belles if they were to get in the habit of wearing false whiskers?"

spot on the crown, about twice the size of a dollar, and we laugh at him for doing so. But may it not be questioned which is the greater object of derision, a bald head or a beardless face? We are also in the habit of ridiculing young ladies because they lace or compress their waists, but would it not be equally becoming in them to sneer at us for disfiguring our faces?

What would we think of the belles if they were to get in the habit of wearing false whiskers? Would we not characterize the introduction of such a fashion as a silly and whimsical innovation? But is it any more ridiculous or censurable in a woman to make her face masculine than it is in a man to make his feminine?

That the beard is a protection against sore throats, coughs, colds, asthma, and other ailments, every California miner will be willing to testify. It is said that the English colliers who have long suffered from hemorrhage of the lungs, have evaded the disease altogether by discontinuing the use of the razor. Yet the newspapers inform us that the clerks in the Bank of England are not allowed to wear mustachios under penalty of dismissal!

CHAPTER ELEVEN

THE LAND OF GOLD

Mₒᵣₑ than satisfied with the experience I had acquired in mining operations in California, I found much difficulty in deciding upon my future course. Before long, however, an old acquaintance and friend earnestly urged me to accompany him to Columbia and take an interest in a very promising mining venture.

My friend said "he felt quite sure that we could make an ounce ($16) a day each with the utmost ease provided we were favored with sufficient rain. And as the rainy season was close at hand, he was fully satisfied that we should have as plentiful a supply of water as our mining operations would require."

I had heard of these diggings frequently and that gold was found there in great abundance, but as no stream watered these surface mines they could only be worked during the rainy season. As my friend's story was corroborated by my own knowledge of these things, I agreed without much hesitation to join him—mentally resolving, however, that it should be the last of my efforts to become suddenly rich by delving for gold in the mines of California.

We left San Francisco in the latter part of the month of October, ran up the river San Joaquin to Stockton in a stern-wheel steamboat so crowded with passengers that berths were entirely out of the question. We were doomed to get through the night as best we could. And such a night! It is my candid belief that this particular night lasted as long as thirteen others combined together. During its continuance I visited the infernal regions upon the pressing invitation of a legion of fiends all wearing Chinamen's hats and long tails. Moreover, I solemnly assert that almost every winged insect and other creeping thing within a circuit of fifty leagues paid their respects to me on board that miserable little steamboat.

I have a faint recollection of invoking the aid of all the saints in the calendar for relief but they would not hear me, and so I e'en concluded to imitate great Caesar's example at the base of Pompey's statue,—wrap my head in my mantle, and thus resign myself to inexorable fate.

As to my friend, I had lost sight of him almost as soon as we entered the boat, and it was great gratification to think that remorse had caused him to commit suicide. After a long and unsuccessful search for him I became sure that he had leaped overboard from sheer shame and conscience for having deluded me into this scrape, and hoped by drowning himself to atone in some measure for his atrocious conduct.

Poor fellow! I forgave him, and mentally resolved to get up something pathetic in shape of an obituary notice as thus:

Departed This Life
October 25th
by water
one
SHAD BACK
(Real name supposed to be Shadrach Bachus)
Aged 34, or thereaway.
The immediate cause of his death was remorse of conscience for having decoyed an unsuspecting and virtuous youth on board a poor miserable craft crowded with passengers, without berths, without seats, and swarming with vermin of every description including Chinamen. It is supposed that in a moment of despair, produced by witnessing the distress of his victim, he jumped into the river and was drowned. His numerous friends cannot but bewail his untimely end although some are of the opinion that it "sarved him right."
Requiescat in pace.

I thought I would add to this a verse or so from some suitable ditty, but could hit upon nothing that would reach the case better than a portion of Gray's Elegy beginning: "Here rests his head upon this lap of earth," etc. Now as I was not fully convinced that "his head did rest upon this lap of earth," I deemed it best to change the text slightly to meet the melancholy occasion and make it read thus:

> There rests beneath the briny wave,
>   A youth to linen and to soap unknown;
> Fair science frowned but failed to save
>   This blessed youth, who then went down.

I confess my inability to state distinctly what is meant by the last line. It seemed to rhyme with "unknown," and as I never had been guilty of an attempt of this kind before, I thought it would do very well as a first effort in poetry. I may as well explain that as I intended to have the whole thing painted on a good sized shingle, and that nailed upon some tree near the sea shore, I thought it would be a good idea to have a hand with an extended finger painted conspicuously on the shingle, to serve as a pointer towards the ocean. This would sufficiently explain the meaning of "there rests," and "briny wave."

Notwithstanding the bodily torments I underwent during that livelong night, with my head wrapped in a mantle and all the rest of my person fairly given over to the mercies of thousands of mosquitos, gnats, sandflies, ants, ticks, fleas and bed-bugs, I really experienced a strong sensation of relief upon reflecting how very handsomely I had disposed of my friend's earthly affairs.

Morning dawned at last and I was in the very act of

gathering the remainder of my person into an upright position, when I heard a voice. It came from beneath an immense heap of Chinamen, Irishmen and niggers, calling me by name and entreating my assistance to get him upon his legs. Deeming it the duty of a good Christian to help a distressed fellow-creature, I made my way through the crowd to the spot whence the voice issued.

There, to my astonishment, I beheld my friend Shad upon his back actively engaged in repelling, with hands and feet, the united assaults of a strong force composed of three Irishmen and four Chinese fellows. Much as I deprecate war in any shape, I could not sufficiently admire the calm appearance of Shad, even when in the heat of the melee. One particular feat performed by one of Shad's feet was observed by me with much astonishment, and it seemed to strike an Irishman very forcibly too, as he honored the performance by immediate prostration.

I proposed mediating between the contending parties, which proposal being acceded to, I forthwith decided the matter in difference, (of which I did not understand one word,) by decreeing a forfeiture of Shad's boots, the restoration of his hat, and the payment by Shad for two gallons of red-eye to regale the company. This last decision was received with marked respect by all but my poor friend.

Peace having been solemnly proclaimed, I had now

an opportunity of better observing my friend Back's personal appearance. He had never been very remarkable for great personal beauty at any period of his life, and the late battle had not left him wholly unscathed. When we came on board of this infernal boat, Mr. Shad Back possessed a pair of bright blue eyes, which had been converted during the night, into a pair of dismal black ones; his nose, always flat, was now scarcely discernible at all—it had been absolutely beaten into his face; lips as thick and black as those of a Loango negro, and without a tooth in his head to save him from starvation.

Although I pitied him truly and sincerely, I could not help feeling a sort of disappointment at knowing he was not drowned or dead in some way. It *was* a great disappointment to me, especially after making extensive preparations to mourn the fate of a man I hoped had committed suicide; after adjusting my face and garments to represent a decent amount of grief; and above all, after composing his epitaph, including therein a scrap of touching poetry, to find that he was not drowned after all. I say again that it *was* a disappointment and a great shame.

We landed in Stockton a little before noon of the same day and took passage in a lumber wagon for Columbia, near which the mines were situated. Columbia is in Tuolumne county near the base of the Sierra Nevada and it contains about 2,000 inhabitants.

Its mines are said to be the richest in the State. As we had come here for the express purpose of making a fortune, we went to work at once, digging and toiling like men determined to become millionaires within a week.

In a few days we had collected a large mass of dirt together and only waited for rain to afford us an opportunity to testing its value. But the rain would not come. Every morning for at least a month Shad predicted rain in torrents, and got drunk without delay in order, as he said, to celebrate an event of so much consequence to our future fortunes.

Sure enough, the rain did come at last. It continued to fall somewhat briskly for about an hour and then it ceased. The amount of water that had fallen barely sufficed to wet the thirsty earth, and it would require just six such rainy days to give us water sufficient to commence our washing operations.

Shad had drunk a more than ordinary quantity of liquor that day, in commemoration, I suppose, of the beginning of the rainy season.

The year previous it had rained for three months without cessation; now we had no rain. December passed away and January had come; men and animals drooped, the earth became baked, not a leaf, not even a blade of grass could be seen in any direction. Shad had been sober for several days upon compulsion entirely. He could get no more liquor for want of

"He had fallen a willing victim to the artful
blandishments of an ancient squaw."

money to pay for it. My own funds were out, gone
to liquidate our daily expenses, so that the prospect
before us looked gloomy enough. Without water to
separate the precious metal from the dirt, we could
do nothing.

The season was now so far advanced that we could
no longer hope for continuous rain, if it came at all,

so I resolved to abandon our pile of gold and make the best of my way back to San Francisco. It was next to impossible to expect aid or counsel from poor Shad. He, good susceptible soul, had fallen a willing victim to the artful blandishments of an ancient squaw. Not so much on account of her great personal attractions as in consequence of her valuable possessions, which consisted of a dilapidated blanket and a keg of whiskey. I was quite charmed with the appearance of the squaw, she so strongly resembled a kangaroo. I found it utterly useless to remonstrate with him. In fact he never was in a fitting condition to understand me, so I made up my mind to leave him.

Through the kindness of a friend, which was afterwards reciprocated, I was enabled to pay the few debts I had contracted and to leave Columbia with a trifle which, with economy, enabled me to reach San Francisco in due time.

Thus terminated my last mining adventure in the gold regions of California.

CHAPTER TWELVE

TRAVAILS WITH
A DONKEY

ONCE more in San Francisco, I made preparations to return to the Atlantic States as rapidly as my health and dilapidated means would permit. But before leaving this pseudo El Dorado forever, I had a wish to see a celebrated grazing district, famed for its vast herds of horned cattle and wild horses. So having hired at an enormous price a sorry looking mule, I sallied forth from San Francisco in search of new adventures. I took the high road along the bay towards Bodega, a small town situated upon the Pacific coast 60 miles north-east from San Francisco.

I had hardly cleared the suburbs of the city when my mule began to exhibit qualities very far from respectable. He would stop suddenly, hold down his head, plant his fore feet firmly and reflect, I suppose, upon the proper moment to pitch me over his head. He had a very uncomfortable way of throwing up his head and more than once just grazed my nose. And he was so playful, jerking the bridle suddenly and casting his head round so as almost to reach my leg with his teeth.

Moreover, I judged him to be partial to botanical studies. He took every opportunity to pushing his way through the scrub bushes that lined the road, as if he thought the occasion favorable to scrape me off his back. I have never been very famous for my skill in equitation, nor have I ever been too anxious to intrust myself to the care and safe-keeping of other legs than my own, and I must acknowledge that when I discovered the little eccentricities already enumerated, I thought it would be most prudent to return. I would have done so, only that the devilish brute would not consent to take the back track.

When I attempted to turn his head homeward, he commenced such a series of circumgyratory evolutions that I remained long in doubt as to which of my limbs would remain unbroken when I did come to the ground. This was a catastrophe by no means far distant if he continued to spin around five minutes longer. I clung to the pummel of the Spanish saddle, however, with the gripe of a maniac, shouting wo! with an unction and vigor.

Any person, to have seen my involuntary performances on this trying occasion, would most assuredly have pronounced me the best circus rider in the known world. I am favorably known at home as even tempered but I verily believe I lost my temper here on this spot. Not that I remember to have ever been profane, but I am sure I consigned the wretch to the safe-keeping of a nameless personage with a particular request regarding his future. As I could do nothing better I let him have his own way, and for the next hour or so we got along very well together.

I really began to think well of his muleship when suddenly, and as if by magic, I found myself upon my back in the road, and the precious villian prancing and curveting within fifty feet of where I lay. I had received a slight bruise upon one of my shoulders and was considering the best method of catching the atrocious robber as he very deliberately walked up to me and adjusted his position so that I could mount him again with ease, which I did without delay.

Soon we reached a Chinese encampment—all men, and they look exactly alike in face and in dress. Two or three were assembled around a fire and the rest were gambling. Those by the fire were engaged in cooking rats. There were about a bushel of these animals altogether, and they were laid with their skins on, from time to time, upon a bed of hot embers to broil. I declined the honor of dining with these Celestials and without much further trouble or delay we arrived, towards midnight, at Bodega.

My mule behaved like a trump during the latter part of the journey, but only after frolicking for about three quarters of an hour up and down a small stream which his excellency insisted upon surveying.

Bodega contains not more than four hundred inhabitants including Digger Indians, niggers and dogs. The last are by far the most useful and most decent of the concern. First settled by the Russians, it recently became the property of an American. Some years ago this man resided in Valparaiso where he married several bags of doubloons, a large lot of cattle, some fine horses, and a Chilian lady.* He then removed to California and became the possessor of the town of Bodega and a very large portion of the surrounding country.

For my part, I could see nothing very seductive there; the country is almost destitute of timber, but well adapted for farming purposes. In fact, it is said to be the best grazing section in the State of California. Dense fogs prevail throughout the summer months and the earth receives sufficient moisture to produce an abundant crop of grass upon which vast herds of cattle and droves of horses are raised. The horned cattle are slaughtered in immense numbers, merely for their horns, hides and tallow.

Twelve miles south-east of Bodega is the little village

---

* It is interesting to note that, shortly after this was written, Helper himself resided in Buenos Aires where he married several bags of doubloons, a large lot of cattle, some fine horses and an Argentine lady.

of Petaluma, situated upon the margin of an extensive swamp through which a small stream winds. It is entirely overflowed during the winter. In the summer it becomes perfectly dry, and cracks open in every imaginable direction to the depth of twelve or fifteen feet, the crevices varying from one to eight inches in width.

If an animal attempts to cross this fissured spot he must assuredly break his legs. It is no uncommon occurrence daily to find three or four wild horses, and as many more horned cattle, vainly struggling to extricate their fractured limbs from the clefts and crevices in this death-dealing Golgotha. In this situation they are quickly dispatched.

Upon my return to Bodega, I witnessed the punishment of an Indian boy for theft. The boy had stolen a trifling sum from the house of an American and he was sentenced to expiate his offense in a very novel manner. The scene reminded me strongly of the main incidents in Lord Byron's "Mazeppa". A wild horse that had been caught with the lasso only the day before was brought out, and the boy's person in an upright position securely strapped to his back. The boy thus bound, the horse was then freed from restraint by the men that held him, and with a cut from a whip, he bounded away.

He had scarcely accomplished a third of a mile,

when he suddenly threw himself, and with frantic efforts endeavored to roll over and over, in order to rid himself of his burden. One of the boy's legs was literally crushed into a bloody mass. The violent exertions of the animal had so far exhausted his strength, that he was unable to rise. In this condition, we had time to come up and liberate the boy from his bonds, but he had ceased to breathe. He was quite dead, and another murder was to be added to the long list of California crimes. Horror-stricken and distressed at the scene of ruthless barbarity I had just witnessed, I made my way out of the village of Bodega.

In returning, I took the road through the valleys of Sonoma and Napa to Benicia. This town contains about 1500 inhabitants and is 40 miles north-east from San Francisco, situated upon a branch of the Sacramento river. It is a port of entry, contains an arsenal, a navy-yard, and extensive docks for repairing and refitting steamers. Ships of the largest class can come up to the wharves. It has been proposed to establish the seat of government of the State here.

Desirous of examining more closely a singularly formed elevation some fifteen miles from Benicia, known as Monte Diabolo, I set out to visit this famous mountain. Mounted upon my rascally mule, I had suffered myself to be persuaded to wear a pair of Spanish spurs. Alleged friends assured me that the hitherto fractious conduct of the mule was entirely owing to not having provided myself with these persuaders before.

I had ridden barely the half of a mile, when the accursed animal was seized with a fiend-like desire to break my neck and his own too. With this purpose in view he began by taking short leaps forward, backward and sideways, varied every now and then by an effort to throw me over his head by casting his hind legs high into the air or by standing almost upright and pawing the air with his fore feet. I maintained my seat with difficulty during these fiendish gambols and plied him with the spurs. This settled the matter at once. No sooner did I plunge the sharp rowels into his infernal sides than he stood for a moment as if to gather strength. Then, dropping his head, he suddenly threw out his hind feet with such violence as to eject me from his back with an impetus that I am astonished did not crush every bone in my body and kill me outright. As it was, my left leg only was broken. The mule, demon as he was, seemed to exult in his misdeeds, and to be well content with the (to him) triumphant termination of the contest. At least I judged so, from his sounding the trumpet of victory long and loud; he brayed incessantly for an hour.

My leg was broken just above the ankle, and whenever I moved it gave me exquisite pain. I didn't know what to do; I couldn't move. I was somewhat comforted, however, by reflecting that I should not lie in this helpless condition long. I was on the highway, and some traveler must pass soon. I shouted with all the voice I had left.

At length I attempted to drag myself upon my hands and knees towards Benicia, then less than a mile distant. In the effort, the agony I endured caused me to faint. When I again returned to consciousness, I found myself in bed, with my broken limb confined between splints.

I received every attention from the kind people into whose hands I had fallen. They had found me insensible by the wayside, my mule standing within ten feet of me, very gravely contemplating his handiwork, afterwards suffering himself to be led back to Benicia, without making the slightest demonstration of discontent. As soon as my new friends discovered the cause of my accident, it was proposed to shoot the mule.

I objected, not from any desire to save his worthless carcass, but from a wish to return him to his more worthless owner in San Francisco, whom I had some hope the animal would cripple for life upon some future day. I therefore requested my friends to have him returned to his owner by the first opportunity that offered.

CHAPTER THIRTEEN

PROVINCIAL
SOCIETY

O<small>F ALL</small> the aborigines that are known to travelers within the limits of the western continent, the Digger Indians are certainly the most filthy and abominable. A worse set of vagabonds cannot be found bearing the human form. Their chief characteristics are indolence and gluttony.

Partially wrapped in filthy rags, with their persons unwashed, hair uncombed and swarming with vermin, they may be seen loitering about the kitchens and slaughter-houses waiting to seize upon and devour like hungry wolves such offal or garbage as may be thrown to them. Grasshoppers, snails and wasps are favorite delicacies with them, and they have a peculiar relish for a certain little animal, which the Bible tells us greatly afflicted the Egyptians in the days of Pharaoh.

The term Digger has been applied to these Indians in consequence of their method of procuring their food. The grasshopper or cricket of California is one of their favorite messes. They capture these insects by first digging a pit in the ground and then forming a wide circle round it which is gradually narrowed. In this manner they drive the insects to the pit and there capture them.

After having secured their prey, the next thing is to prepare it for food. This is accomplished either by baking the grasshoppers in the fire or drying them in the sun, after which the Diggers pulverize them. The epicures among them crush service-berries into a jam and thoroughly incorporate the pulverized insects with the pulpy mass to which they have reduced the fruit. Others mix their cricket meal with parched sunflower seed, but this is an advance in civilization and in the luxuries of the table which is made by very few of them. They obtain the young wasps by burning the grass, which exposes the nests and enables them to grub in the earth for this delicacy.

Acorns are also a favorite article of diet with these wretched creatures. In California this fruit is larger and more palatable than with us. They pound them. up, mix them with wild fruit and make their meal into a sort of bread. They are said to resort to a stratagem to obtain the acorns in greater abundance. There is a bird in California called the carpenteir or carpenter. He busies himself in making holes in the redwood trees and filling them with acorns. When a Digger finds a tree stocked in this manner, he kindles a fire at its base, (so the story goes,) and keeps it up till the tree falls, when he helps himself to the acorns. Grass-seed constitutes another portion of their diet. This is gathered by the women and made into bread.

It is reported on good authority that Captain Sutter, at whose fort (the present site of Sacramento) gold was first discovered, employed these people to build his fort for him. He paid them in tin coins of his own invention upon which was stamped the number of days the holder had worked. This was taken at his "store" for articles of merchandise.

He fed his Indians upon the offal of slaughtered animals and the bran sifted from ground wheat. The latter was boiled in large iron kettles, and then placed in wooden troughs from which they scooped it out with their hands. They are said to have eaten it with great relish.

These Indians are inveterate gamblers, and when they have been so fortunate as to obtain clothing, they are almost sure to gamble it away till they reduce themselves to the costume of Adam.

When pinched by the severity of hunger and unable to procure their customary filthy diet, they are driven to the settlements where they steal if they can and do a little labor if they must.

CHAPTER FOURTEEN

ARE YOU GOING
TO CALIFORNIA?

In the preceding chapters it has been my purpose to impart such information as would lead my reader to a correct knowledge of the present condition of things in California and to aid him in deciding whether he will emigrate to that country or content himself in the Atlantic States. I have endeavored (in a very brief and feeble manner, it is true) to purge the films from his eyes, that he might see the country in its true light.

I have told the reader of the distorted and exaggerated stories which have been circulated concerning it; of its barren soil, and unfavorable seasons; of the seeming incompleteness of nature, and the paucity of resources of employment therein; of its scanty productions, and dependence upon importations for all kinds of provisions and merchandise; of the expensiveness of living, and the extraordinary obstacles which lie in the way of prosecuting business with success; of the unprecedented number of mishaps and accidents, and the losses and perils to be apprehended from fire and water; of the lack of scenery, and the disagreeable consequences of the weather; of the inefficiency of the laws, and the anarchical state of society; of the breaches of faith between man and wife—of the almost utter disregard of the marriage relation, and the unexampled debauchery and lewdness of the community; of the contrariety of opinions which prevail, and the continual disputes and disturbances which arise in consequence of the heterogeneousness of the population.

Furthermore, I have informed my readers of the servile employments to which learned and professional men have to resort for the means of subsistence, the thousands of penniless vagabonds who wander about in misery and dejection; of the dissipated and desperate habits of the people, and the astounding number of suicides and murders; of the incessant brawls and tumults, and the popularity of dueling; of the arbitrary doings of mobs, and the supremacy of lynch-law; of the general practice of carrying deadly weapons, and the contempt that is shown for human life; of the great difficulty of securing reliable titles to landed property, and the fatal rencounters with the squatters; of the bacchanalian riots by day, and the saturnalian revels at night; of the perfidy and delinquency of public functionaries, and the impossibility of electing an honest man to office; of the sophistication of provisions, and the filthy fare in hotels and restaurants; of the untrustworthy character of business men, and the frauds and stratagems practiced in almost every transaction; of the contemning of religious sentiments, and the desecration of the Sabbath; of the incendiaries in the cities, and the banditti in the mountains; of the alarming depravity of the adolescent generation—of the abominable dissoluteness of many of the women—the infamous vices of the men, and the flagitious crimes against nature.

I have spoken freely of all these things, and now what else shall I say? Is it necessary that I should defile still more paper with these detestable truths? Can any one be still in a state of indecision about going to California? I am aware that the public mind has been somewhat undecided upon this subject and I have essayed to give it the proper turn or restore it to equilibrium. I have spread facts before my reader and have related events which occurred under my own observation.

There are scores of other topics which might be brought in to give strength to my general argument. I will now lay before the reader a few extracts from letters which I have recently received from friends in the Pacific State and it will be seen how fully they corroborate my own statement.

An editorial friend, writing to me recently from San Francisco, says:—

"Business all over California remains in the same stagnant condition and every sign prognosticates a time of hardship and suffering. A crisis is approaching which will drag down nine-tenths of the business houses in the country. Money gets more stringent every day and every body seems to be at a loss to know what to do. I must confess I see nothing promising in the future. It is truly a dark day for California."

Another correspondent says:—

"Heaven only knows what is to become of our people. Our markets continue distressingly dull. A great many failures have taken place and others are anticipated. Indeed these are trying times with the mercantile portion of our community. Every thing wears a dull and unpromising aspect. Hundreds of mechanics and laborers in a deplorably destitute condition are sauntering about the streets with nothing to do and unable to find employment. And as a consequence of this unprosperous state of things, we have to contend with many cases of despair and desperation. Within the last week four suicides, three murders, numerous robberies and other crimes have been committed in our city and the accounts from the up-country towns and the interior convince us that there is less respect paid to the moral and civil laws in those places than there is here. Our cities are filled with secret organizations for rapacity and plunder. You have no idea of the number of young men who are getting themselves into a bad pickle by coming to this country. Two earthquakes and several fires have occurred since I wrote to you from Sacramento. The earthquakes were very slight and little damage resulted from them, but the losses by fire have been immense."

And now listen to what the District Attorney for the county of San Francisco says. In a speech which he delivered some time ago in a criminal case in the city of San Francisco he makes use of the following language:—"Twelve hundred murders have been committed in this city within the last four years, and only one of the murderers has been convicted!" What a striking comment is this upon California justice!

If additional evidences of the corruption and rottenness of affairs in California are required, all that is necessary is to look into the papers that come from that State. And let me add that it is impossible to get at the real, naked facts from the California journals. Almost every newspaper in the State is under the control of interested parties and they will not allow the truth to be spoken when it conflicts with their schemes and projects. Nevertheless, enough may be learned from them to convince any reasonable person of the correctness of my description of California.

Thus, then, I have given a fair and truthful statement of what I saw, and those who are not yet convinced must go and test the matter for themselves. They will find what I have told them to be true and

"Law is a nullity, order does not exist."

that there is more enormity there than I have ventured to detail.

The absence of all social feeling, of refinement, of the little elegancies of life, is painfully manifest. Law is a nullity, order does not exist except where the dread of the bowie knife or the revolver enforces it. Men of notoriously bad character are intrusted with the management of affairs and are easily accessible to bribery. Justice is proverbially venal, legislation is utterly corrupt.

We have called attention to the general barrenness of the soil and endeavored to impress upon the reader's mind a conviction of the great uncertainties of mining. What then remains to attract the emigrant? The feverish excitement of speculation, which entices so many only to destroy them, especially in California, where projects are pursued with a recklessness elsewhere unknown and losses are on a gigantic scale. What wonder, then, that suicides are so common in that unhappy country?

Of the condition of females in that State, it is useless for me to speak. I have already said enough on that subject and it becomes every man who thinks of emigrating thither to ponder well the risks to which he will subject the ladies of his family. The enormities chargeable upon California in this respect would be difficult to parallel in any age of the world. They are of so gross a nature that it is impossible even to allude to them in a book which may be seen by women.

And now, after having well considered all these things, after having become thoroughly acquainted with the facts I have been at the pains to collect and record, I would again ask my reader, Are you going to California?

THE END.